GRACE'S STORY

Grace Lucas aged 22

Grace's Story

*Growing up in Herne Hill during the
First World War*

Grace MacFarquhar
née Lucas

Edited by
Laurence Marsh and Colin Wight

THE HERNE HILL SOCIETY

First published 2018
by the Herne Hill Society
PO Box 27845
London SE24 9XA

Book design by Sophia Marsh
Cover illustration by Laurence Marsh

The Herne Hill Society is grateful to the following for the use of images:

Elizabeth Sirriyeh and Frankie Maclean, frontispiece and illus. 5, 10, 17, 18, 38, 41, 42 and 43
Lambeth Archives, illus. 2 and 25
Imperial War Museum, illus. 20
Robin Drayton, illus. 31
William Corbett-Winder, illus. 33 and 35
The National Trust, illus. 36
King's College London, illus. 39

ISBN 978-0-9540323-3-3

CONTENTS

FOREWORD

As we mark the centenary of the end of the First World War this year, there is an urgency to our remembrance, to capturing and disseminating the oral histories of those who lived through the war, and who can speak first hand of its horrors and of the impact that it had, both at home and abroad. The story of the war is easily described in statistics and place names, but it is of course the story of millions of individuals and families whose lives were interrupted, changed for ever and often devastated as a consequence. These personal stories have a unique power to help us remember, and to motivate us to work for peace.

Grace's Story is vivid and moving, her personality speaks from the page, and her clear recollection of details – both of her surroundings and human interactions – bring her account to life. Grace tells not only of the impact of the war, but more generally of life in South London during the early part of the 20th century, and the immense challenges her mother faced as a war widow with a large family to support.

While it is hard now to imagine anti-aircraft guns firing from Ruskin Park, it is essential that we do so, to honour the generation who lived through that time and fought and gave their lives, to appreciate fully the peace and freedom that we currently enjoy, and to ensure that we don't take it for granted.

The Herne Hill Society's "Remembering Herne Hill 1914-18" project is hugely exciting, helping school-age children living in Herne Hill to understand what the war was like for children just like them, living on the same streets, at that time. It is also a fitting memorial to all those from our local area who had the course of their lives irrevocably changed by the war, and whose courage and resilience were so remarkable. Grace's moving account helps us to honour them.

Helen Hayes MP
Member of Parliament for
Dulwich and West Norwood
November 2018

Introduction

The scale of the destruction and loss of human life caused by the First World War still shocks a century later. Of the 10-11 million combatants who died worldwide, about eight percent were from the United Kingdom. It has been estimated that some 100,000 Londoners were killed and 230,000 wounded. These figures are almost incomprehensible; but it is the stories of individual suffering that stay in our memories.

St Saviour's Church, in Herne Hill Road, was demolished in 1981 but a memorial tablet survives.[1] It includes the name F LUCAS. In the course of research for our Lottery-funded project "Remembering Herne Hill 1914-18", we began to look into this soldier's life and death. He did not initially show up

1. *St Saviour's memorial (left hand panel)*

2. *St Saviour's memorial (central section)*

as a soldier from Herne Hill because the Commonwealth War Graves Commission, while recording his details and an address at 45 Kemerton Road, had this as an address in Camberwell. One hundred years ago there was no unanimity as to which London area Kemerton Road belonged to. The same debate can be heard today. We make no apology for claiming this to be a story about growing up in Herne Hill because it was clearly the view of Grace, the writer of this memoir, that she thought of the area of her childhood as Herne Hill. At the same time her experiences also embraced Camberwell, Loughborough Junction and Brixton – and places away from London.

The soldier on the St Saviour's Memorial was Fred Lucas, father of Grace, the eldest of five children, and husband of Charlotte. We were most fortunate that our research trail led to two of Fred's grandchildren and other descendants with an interest in preserving his legacy. So it was that we found not merely far more detail about Fred's life than we would have expected, but we were able to see a period of history vividly brought to life through the eyes and in the words of a young girl who lived through it.

Grace's account of her father's death in 1916 – and the consequences for her widowed mother – was, no doubt, a story repeated with minor variations in thousands of London homes. Suddenly, everything changed. No more singing and dancing in the kitchen. It is not "the big picture" but the mundane details of survival, such as Lottie Lucas at Brixton market on a Saturday evening hoping to get a cheap joint of meat and a few vegetables to feed the family, or struggling into town on the tram from Camberwell Green with five young children to petition for a pension, that bring home the brutal change of circumstances faced by so many families.

Grace also remembers lighter moments – parties in the family home with music hall entertainers from impresario Fred Karno's troupe, along with members of the theatrical Lupino family. She draws a vivid portrait of the arrogant and unpopular (certainly with Grace's mother) Revd Bayfield Clark and other local figures – such as shopkeepers and the teachers at St Saviour's primary school. There are descriptions of holiday escapes to Paulerspury in Northamptonshire, Thaxted in Essex and, surprisingly, Vaynor Park, a country estate in Montgomeryshire. And there are the simple ups and downs, remembered with affection, of sharing a home with four siblings.

The story continues after the war, with Grace obliged to abandon her ambition to go to art college under pressure to get a sensible job and put food on the family table. She enters the Civil Service and does well.

Time passes and memories are lost. How often one hears it said, "If only I had asked my parents, or grandparents or great aunt about…" In preparing Grace's story for publication that thought has often occurred to us. Yet we have the reward of her memories living on and the prospect of their now reaching many more people through this book.

Grace wrote down her memories towards the end of her life, seven decades after the events she describes. Not surprisingly, we have found that she got some things wrong – though whether this is because she once had a more accurate recollection or because she always had a "false memory" is impossible to say. And if that was always her recollection, is it false? For example, she says her father's mother was French. That was not the case, but she clearly believed it to be true. One suspects that it was something Grace was once told and liked to believe. We have therefore provided detailed notes which explore issues of accuracy and which, more generally, give some additional background.

Frederick Lucas was not the typical casualty of the war. In the first place he was older, born on 4 September 1879 – 34 years of age when the war broke out, 10 or more years older than most of those who flocked to join the "New Army". Fred came from a family with its roots in the industrial processes that helped forge the wealth of Victorian England. Other branches of the family appear to have profited from that wealth, but very little came the way of Fred growing up in South London. He was born in Peckham, the third of nine children of Edward Henry and Caroline Lucas. The street has disappeared with redevelopment but would have comprised small terraced houses, probably shared by two families. Fred's father (1853-1905) was an "engine fitter and turner", but unusual in that there are family accounts of his also being an artist and occasionally making money in that way. The 1891 Census shows the family, including 11-year-old Fred, now living in Sayer Street. It disappeared entirely with the building of the Heygate Estate at the Elephant and Castle, itself now replaced by gleaming new blocks of flats. A world away from Sayer Street where families were often wretchedly poor and living in grossly overcrowded conditions.

It seems clear that Fred's family was going down in the world. Fred's answer was to leave home as soon as he could. He joined the Army, claiming he was over 18 when he was in truth only 17, but the Royal Artillery seems not to have been concerned. In 1899 he was sent out with his unit, the 4th Battery of the Royal Field Artillery, to South Africa, serving throughout the Second Boer War. He left the Army in 1904, and the following year married Charlotte Finch at St John's Church, West Ealing. Her family background was also one of South London poverty. Grace, the first of their five children, was born in 1906, followed over the next eight years by Dorothy, Gladys, Fred and Vera.

The Metropolitan Police were keen to have former soldiers among their ranks, provided their disciplinary record was good, and for two years Fred served as a Police Constable. He was "permitted to resign", which may be a polite way of saying that he was required to do so, but the exact circumstances are not known. The growing family lived in various parts of London before settling in Herne Hill by about 1913. Fred was by now established in business as a motor engineer in one of the many railway arches around Loughborough Junction. These were the days when small local workshops could build cars from scratch – the "Croxted" was produced around this time in a Herne Hill workshop off Croxted Road. And Grace remembers a car built for the family by her father, though a photograph of it with the family aboard has been lost.

Fred's later "attestation papers" (papers that record enlistment and military record) have not survived. It seems that he rejoined at an early stage – before conscription was introduced – this time the Army Ordnance Corps, who were no doubt keen to have his mechanical skills. The account that has been passed down the family is that Fred was initially attached to the armament makers Vickers at Crayford in Kent. Their main product here was the deadly Maxim machine gun, the invention of Hiram Maxim (at one time pursuing his dangerous experiments in the garden of his home in Norwood Road). On the back of the portrait photograph (see Illustration 17) that Fred sent to his sister Annie at Christmas 1915 he wrote: "Just doing a little bit more for the old country. I'm going out to France on the 10th". The "little bit" that Fred did included devising technical improvements for the heavy siege howitzer known as "Mother" and possibly also for tanks, then in their infancy. The award of the Military Medal to Fred may well be linked to the special skills he was able to provide.

3. *Royal Artillery Memorial with heavy siege howitzer (see Note 14)*

Staff Serjeant Fred Lucas died in the fourth week of the four and a half months' attrition known as the Battle of the Somme, a battle that saw more than one million killed and wounded. Fred is thought to have been the victim of gassing and was taken to the XIV Corps Main Dressing Station. Here he died on 23 July 1916 and was buried nearby in the Dive Copse British Cemetery at Sailly-le-Sec, 12 miles to the east of Amiens.

Laurence Marsh & Colin Wight
November 2018

GRACE'S STORY

My parents Fred and Charlotte Lucas

The earliest memory I have of my father is in the summer of 1913. I was seven years old, and going on a Sunday School outing with about 20 small children. We were going by train from Herne Hill and in order to get to the Station we had to pass my father's workshops which were under the railway arches. My father was an engineer, and across the doors in large letters was the legend F. LUCAS, ENGINEER AND MOTOR BODY BUILDER. He was standing at the open door of the workshop and gave each one of us a halfpenny. You could buy a large bag of sweets for a halfpenny in those days. Herne Hill at this time was in Surrey and practically surrounded by fields and orchards. It is now London SE24, with housing estates all over the fields.

Father was a tall, handsome man, cheerful and with many friends, particularly in the theatrical world. He maintained and repaired the coaches that transported the music hall troupes, with all their costumes and goods, from town to town. They often slept in the coaches when they could not afford digs. The Lupino family[2] were the group I remember best. There were parties in our house too. A young actor with the impossible name of Oscar Golightly played the piano and the rest talked, and sang and drank. The next day my mother would grumble at the rings made by the beer glasses on her highly polished tables.

4. *Stanley Lupino in 1919*

During these parties my sister Dorothy and I were supposed to be in bed, but we crept down and sat on the bottom of the stairs trying not to be noticed. Dorothy was a year younger than me: very pretty with golden curls and deep-set blue eyes. I was thin, skinny with, I expect, my hair in plaits. I remember being very upset one evening when one of the chorus girls caught up Dorothy and carried her round the room singing "My great big beautiful doll", which was a hit at the time.

We loved going to my father's workshops, with the machinery making a lot of noise and smelling of oil and lathes and tools all over the place. One day we went down to see a mongrel dog and its puppies. When my father had found it and installed it in the corner of his workshop it had been named Bob, but now it had produced six puppies she became Bobess! I was wearing my new muff, white, with little black tails on it. I stuffed one of the puppies into my muff and managed to get it home before it was discovered! I was in trouble on two counts: one, the puppy had made a mess in my new muff, and two, I had almost suffocated the poor thing! I seemed to be one of those children that was always in trouble.

5 *Charlotte Lucas, Grace's mother, as a young woman*

Often I got a belting from my father for telling lies. I was a great storyteller and would amuse my sisters Dorothy and Gladys by telling them about the beautiful dresses we had in the cupboard and the holiday by the sea we were going to have, with buckets and spades. I knew it was all make-believe but one of my sisters asked Mother if she could wear the red velvet dress in the cupboard, or when we were going to the seaside! When my father came home he was told about my wicked storytelling, and off would come his belt and I would get a strapping. The cane lived on a hook at the back of the kitchen door and my brother could reach it any time. It was a little whippy thing with a handle and could be bought at the general shop on the comer for a halfpenny. It was usually my brother or myself that were due for the cane, and as my brother broke it in half if he possibly could, it became part of the punishment to buy our own cane. I always said it was for him and he said it was for me! The shopkeeper was fat and jolly and – with everything under the sun – he sold little paper storybooks for a farthing and always gave us one with the cane. My sister Dorothy was very sweet and gentle and rather delicate, and was very rarely in trouble, and Gladys was rather chubby and only four. My brother Fred was three, very active and mischievous, and myself, aged seven, telling stories to amuse the others, which qualified me for punishment. I preferred the belt to the cane. My father himself was a writer, writing articles for engineering magazines. Also he was an avid reader of Dickens and Shakespeare, and I rather feel he sympathised with another storyteller.

Occasionally on a fine summer afternoon we were taken for a ride in Father's car. I had a photo of such an outing, my father had made the car and I think it went up to the extraordinary speed of 10 miles an hour. My father sat at the steering wheel, smoking a pipe and wearing a deerstalker hat, rather like Sherlock Holmes was supposed to wear. Mother sat next to him with a motor veil tied firmly over a little black hat, which sat jauntily on top of her wonderful mass of dark auburn hair. She wore her hair in a great coil in the nape of her neck but it was always falling down her back. Father used to say she was a "hank of hair and a bundle of rags" as often, after dressing four active children, she put on the nearest thing that came to hand – which had often seen better days! However, she was lovely, with that creamy matt skin which sometimes goes with auburn hair. She was also emotional with a quick temper. We all kept out of her way when her temper flared! Perched on a kind of form at the back of the car, my sister Dorothy and I hung on rather precariously. We had on our best Sunday dresses, white silk with frills round the edge of the skirt and the puff sleeves. Our hats were of a stiff organdy with the brim all crimped with the goffering iron.[3] Mother used these goffering irons for all kinds of things, includ-

6 *Jolly Book Annual 1913*

ing my hair when we were invited to a party! It did not suit me and I was always most embarrassed. The car had no hood or screen so we only went out in it on a fine day. We were the envy of all our school friends.

My father was very good with us children. On Sunday we had a roast midday dinner and my father would carve – it was usually a large joint of beef. He would go round the table asking us what we wanted. If we said "sausages" he carved slices of beef and said "there you are, sausages" and we were perfectly happy. At Christmas we had a doll or a book. Dorothy had an annual called *Chatterbox*, and I had one called the *The Jolly Book*. Gladys always asked for a doll. One Christmas brother Fred had a railway set with an engine and two carriages which you wound up with a key, and they went round and round. All our friends were invited to see it. We made a lot of our own toys. Mother often bought a Weldon's fashion catalogue which had patterns for all the family. We cut out the models and stuck

them on cardboard

7 Weldon fashion catalogue, 1910

with tabs on the back to make them stand up. Then we made a theatre from a cardboard box and I wrote extraordinary plays for them to act. From another large box my father made a doll's house. We made curtains from scraps of material and furni-ture from chestnuts, spent matches, matchboxes and cardboard. It kept us from out of our mother's way for hours – even if we did quarrel over who did what and whose was the best. Dorothy and I wrote the most peculiar plays and our friends came up to the playroom while we acted them to our long-suffering mothers.

We had no television or radio in those days, so on Sundays our friends would come in and we would gather round the piano to sing songs. My father had a magic lantern, and all the children would sit round to watch this won-

8 Grace's home at Kemerton Road (photo 2018)

derful show. On the whole we enjoyed our small pleasures.

At the top of the house[4] there was a long room which became our playroom. In it was the water tank which made the most awful noise, so it could not be used as another bedroom. It had a big table covered with a bake cloth, which had innumerable stains on it, and a fireplace where we roasted chestnuts on a shovel with holes in it. It is a wonder we did not burn the house down. The coals we brought up from the dining room coal-scuttle, and the matches we found in the kitchen – and hid them! Mother never worried about what went on in this room. We were supposed to keep it tidy and clear up any mess we made, which we did as far as our limited abilities allowed. At the end of the garden was a row of chestnut trees; we picked the nuts up from the ground.

Mother's name was Charlotte, and she loved beautiful things about her. Often we visited the second-hand shops where the dealer would keep a special table or chair for her. If it was broken or dilapidated my father mended it for her and then she polished it until it shone. I still have a little footstool with its original tapestry cover and lovely mahogany feet. When she was in a particularly good mood she would sing all the old music hall songs for us and we would trot round the room chanting "Doing the Lambeth Walk".[5] It was quite possible that the next morning one of us would upset her, and Gabriel and all his archangels could not please her. We would all be in trouble, and it was at those times that we would go up to our room and try not to be noticed.

My sister Dorothy would let us know if all was well or if there was likely to be a meal for us. Even my father did not escape her temper. One day he brought home some photographs someone had taken of him – perhaps one of his girl admirers, because she threw a cup of tea at him and the photographs, destroying them completely. He probably went to his workshop until all was well again.

My mother's upbringing had been very erratic.[6] Her father was drowned before she was born, and her mother had a small factory making artificial flowers where she employed a few young girls with skilled fingers. Artificial flowers were very much in vogue in those days.

The older women, who were likely no more than 40 years old, wore little bonnet-shaped hats, with a bunch of artificial violets on the front. It would also seem to have been the fashion to wear little shoulder capes, sometimes decorated with sequins.

A young woman named Grace Godfrey worked in my grandmother's shop. She had a house left to her by her father and a small private income. She probably did not have to earn her living but would have enjoyed the work in the flower shop. Grace was some years older than my mother but she befriended the young girl who often came into the shop after school and amused herself among the coloured tissue and bits of bright silks. Grace remained my mother's good friend for many years. She was my mother's bridesmaid when she married, and when I was born she promised to leave me her house and possessions if I was named after her. So I was called Grace. My second name, Isabelle, was my father's French mother's name, and also his sister's name.[7]

Another good friend to my mother was her grandfather. He was a big burly Scot named John Boyd, and he was a buyer of horses for Thomas Tilling's buses. These buses had two big dray horses to pull them, and the top deck was open. You could ride all through London for a halfpenny. John Boyd drove around in a pony and trap, often taking Mother with him to the horse fairs.

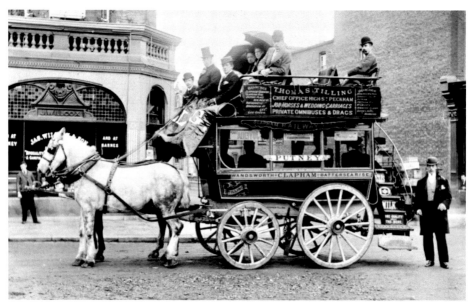

9 *Thomas Tilling horse bus*

He was a cheerful and God-fearing man, going to Church on Sundays wearing his kilt, but he was also a heavy drinker. One day, after a busy day at one of the horse fairs, and possibly after drinking with his many friends, he fell down the stairs and broke his neck. So my mother lost her good friend.

My grandmother married again, to a man named Fletcher. He was a ganger or a foreman of a party of workmen, and apparently drank rather a lot. He was a bully, and I do not think my mother cared much for her stepfather. He was Irish and a Catholic. His two daughters by a previous marriage went to a convent school, to which my mother was sent. She was so terrified of the ladies in black that they had to take her away.

My grandmother died when my mother was 13. Her stepsister Lillian was much older than her, and married with two children of her own. My mother was taken from school and put to work in a laundry where she earned two shillings a week.[8] This was paid to her stepsister for her keep. Later she got a job as a barmaid but found it quite difficult to keep customers at bay. In those days it was usual for women to go into a public house unless they were streetwalkers.

10 *Charlotte Lucas in stage costume*

Later she became a small-time actress, taking minor parts in musicals. I have a delightful photo of her as the "Belle of New York".[9] This was probably how my father met her, through his theatrical friends.

One of their friends was Fred Karno, who had a troupe of dancing girls that were well known all over the country.[10] Another was a popular music hall singer named Lottie Collins.[11] Mother used to sing many of her songs to us. The manager of the Drury Lane Theatre was another friend, so we had free tickets for the pantomime for many years.

I think we must have been fairly well off, in spite of the money owed to us by my father's theatrical

11 Fred Karno's companies in front of the "Fun Factory" in Southwell Road in 1907

friends, because as well as a beautifully furnished house and a motor car, we had a maidservant. Her name was Mabel Gain. She earned two shillings and sixpence a week, as well as her meals and two white aprons. One of these had frills on for Sundays, the other one was plain for everyday use. She was absolutely no use in the house; I remember her sitting amongst the sticks and coals

12 Poster for Lottie Collins and her most famous song

crying her eyes out because the fire would not light. I was nine years old then and often lighted it for her. She was, however, absolutely marvellous with us children, playing games and singing to us. She was the only person who could get my brother to sleep – she sang to him "Little brown jug, don't I love thee".

In February 1914 my sister Vera was born. Auntie Lil came to mind us while my mother was in bed with the new baby. She was my mother's step-sister, very tall and very severe looking. She regarded us as Charlotte's unruly children and we were a little nervous of her. The first thing she did was to march us all into the bedroom to see the new baby. When

we saw my mother in bed Dorothy and Gladys started to cry and my brother screamed at the top of his voice. They were sent out of the room and I was asked if I would like to hold the baby. I took one look at the little bundle lying next to my mother, and ran.

Poor Auntie Lil. Each morning she was up at 5 a.m. to light the fire for the copper to do all the extra washing for the baby and four children. The girls wore white dresses over their dark winter dresses, and Auntie Lil decided we needed a clean one each day, whereas we normally wore the same one all week, changing on Sundays. She looked after my mother and the baby and cooked our meals while Mabel Gain and her friend Rosie English took us all to the little Church school round the corner, helped in the house, and put us all to bed. The headmistress of the school took my young brother, as she liked my parents and knew he was difficult to manage. Often she sent for me to take him home as the young teacher in the infants class found him too difficult to handle. He was only three, and more than a little jealous of the new baby. One day when Auntie Lil went down to the cellar to fetch coal for the kitchen range Fred bolted the door after her. She banged and banged until Mother had to get out of bed to let her out. I think she went home after that! What I chiefly remember about her was her red flannel petticoats and long lace-up boots. When she crossed the road and lifted up her skirts out of the mud and manure we giggled at the sight of her red petticoat Our mother wore white ones with frills round the bottom and button-up boots, which she took a long while doing up with a button-hook. We

13 *Lord Kitchener*

seemed to muddle through quite well, and on Sunday afternoons we went for walks with mother pushing the bassinette,[12] Dorothy and Gladys on either side, with me at the back holding my brother. The park was closed to us now, as the soldiers had taken it over with their guns and the daily marching of yet more and more young boys awkwardly holding a rifle and being shouted at by the Sergeant Major. I do not think we had a very normal upbringing but we grew like Topsy, without noticing all the talk of war and the shouting of the politicians until suddenly war was declared. Then there were posters everywhere of Lord Kitchener with his arm stretched out, his finger pointing, with the slogan "Your Country Needs You".[13]

August 1914 – The Outbreak of War

Long queues formed outside the recruiting offices all over the country. There were young men, and not so young men, and much-too-young men trying to look older. Some were well-groomed and wearing smart well-tailored suits or country tweeds. There were working men in their Sunday suits and many shabby and hungry men hoping for a shilling a day and Army food. There were

14 *London August 1914, Whitehall Recruitment Office*

hundreds of undergraduates giving up their pacifism and idealistic views to join Kitchener's Army to fight the dreaded Germans. In four long years of war we lost the flower of the nation's youth and I do not think we ever recovered from it. Many of the young men had a long wait to join the Army. They had to go through a stiff medical examination, then collect their clothing, sign on and receive the King's Shilling. Regular Army soldiers went up and down the queues picking out the unlikely, and sending the young boys home to mother. The Salvation Army was busy: young women distributing cups of tea and later setting up soup kitchens. The band played.

Then it was the turn of the women. Young women from all classes of society volunteered to become nurses, ambulance drivers and munitions workers. Then we had postwomen and women tram drivers. In fact nearly every job that had previously been done by an able-bodied young man was now done by a young woman. They found they enjoyed their new-found importance. Many men were already doing work vital to the war effort and were not expected to join the Army. Among these were, of course, the farmers. Retired and experienced men, including Army officers, were called back into service.

Cartoonists had a wonderful time. The newspapers and magazines showed gruesome pictures of fierce Germans wearing spiked helmets with blood dripping from bayonets or pictures of young German soldiers goose-stepping over Belgium. We children did not have newspapers or magazines, but the placards on the

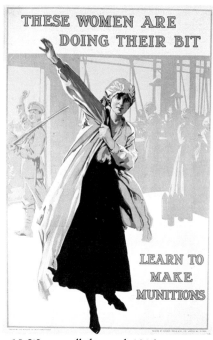

15 *Women called to work 1916*

hoardings in the streets showed lurid pictures of Germans committing the most awful atrocities, which caused us to have nightmares. I was always dreaming of

16 *A poster published in Ireland 1915*

Germans in spiked helmets climbing in through the windows with daggers clenched between their teeth. My sister Gladys was most affected. She started sleepwalking and twice fell down the stairs. One night she knocked over a basin and a jug of cold water, which was on the washstand ready for our early morning wash. There was no hot and cold running water in those days. You washed in cold water, trying to avoid hurting your chilblains. Friday was bath night. We had a big zinc bath in front of the kitchen range, which had a kettle of water boiling, ready to heat the tub up for the next body. A clothes-horse was placed round the bath with towels and nightdresses draped on them. My brother was last. He was lifted in and scrubbed by Mabel Gain, always screaming that he would not go into the bath after all those girls. On thinking back I do not blame him.

Then one day my father came home with his papers. He had joined Kitchener's Army. Being an engineer he was put in the Army Ordnance Corps. He became an artificer on the big gun called "mother". It is now in the Imperial War Museum.[14] It was not a very sophisticated gun; when it was fired it sometimes recoiled and wounded members of its own crew. My father invented something to stop this happening. Being in the Army he could not patent his invention, but he was awarded a decoration and he had a letter from Vickers offering him a big job after the war. I have been told by friends that he made in the Army, particularly a young officer named Captain Coe, that my father had something to do with various refinements on the first tanks. I have no idea what

17 Fred Lucas in uniform c1915, inscribed to his sister Annie. The only known photo of him.

they were but think they were probably something to do with their guns. Tanks were in their very early days.

Mother started to take a daily newspaper at this time, crying over the casualty lists and worrying so much that she became more and more emotional. We were always in trouble, and therefore when we were not at school we spent all our time up in the playroom.

We had a walled garden, which was my mother's great joy. The end wall looked over Ruskin Park.[15] Where we

18 Annie Lucas (1886-1971), sister of Fred Lucas

at one time sat on it to watch the boys playing cricket, we now watched those same boys, in ill-fitting khaki uniforms and carrying rifles, marching round the Park and being shouted at by a Sergeant Major. They were marched around a few times and then sent off to France. Many of them did not come back. Jack Crawford and Will Scenling were 17 – older brothers of our friends.[16] They went off to France. A fortnight later their parents had the dreaded orange telegram to say their sons had been killed. My father said the young boys were just cannon fodder.

1915 – Bombs and No Butter

When German aircraft came over to drop their bombs on London there was no mechanical air raid alarm.[17] Instead a young man who lived next door to us and

was too delicate to enlist as a fighting man, was made an air raid warden. As the planes came over he rode around the streets on a bicycle shouting "take cover" through a loud hailer. After the raid was over he went round again

19 London policemen with air raid warnings

shouting "all clear". The anti-aircraft guns on the park were firing[18] – I am not sure that they knew what they were firing at – but we children all thought it was very exciting, except Gladys who screamed at the top of her voice. My brother and I went to the top of the house where we could see the shells bursting and searchlights weaving round the sky. Then one exciting night we saw a great airship in the sky surrounded by bursting shells and searchlights. Suddenly it burst into flames and came down slowly enveloped by fire. It was the invention of Graf von Zeppelin and named after him. I have never forgotten the sight of that beautiful airship surrounded by flames; even the guns stopped firing and it went very quiet.[19]

Every morning I was told to wait until the postman came in case there was a letter from my father. It was very seldom that a letter came, but one day in March a letter did come, and in it was a card for my birthday. It was very pretty,

embroidered silk with little flowers and the words "forget me not". On the back my father had written in pencil "when you are a big girl you can rub this out and send it to your sweetheart". I kept the card until last year when I sent it to the Imperial War Museum, as I noticed they had similar

20 *Contemporary Zeppelin cartoon, caption below*

MISTRESS (coming to maid's room as the Zeppelins approach): "Jane! Jane! Won't you come downstairs with the rest of us?"
LITTLE MAID: "Oh, thank you, Mum, but I can see beautiful from here, Mum."

cards there. The Keeper of the Art Department sent me the history of these cards. They were embroidered in a convent and sent to the NAAFI as they found they were immensely popular among the soldiery.

In June of 1915 my father came home on leave and it was a marvellously happy time for us all. It was quite surprising how many of his friends knew that he was home and our house was full of their comings and goings and my mother never seemed to mind the beer glass rings on her tables or the piano and singing and dancing.

As the year wore

21 *The sort of silk embroidered card Grace would have received from her father*

on food became more and more scarce. There was no rationing; you could get food on the black market if you had money. My mother had what was called a "separation allowance". It was not very much and the bank balance was getting very low. Then it was announced that inspectors were going round to check on food hoarding. We children lived very well that week as some of our better-off neighbours kept coming round with pots of jam, tins of food or potatoes saying "Would your children like some jam?" Butter seemed to be particularly short and sometimes my mother spread the toast with lard, sprinkling sugar on top if she had some. It was good training as it taught us to eat everything, which I do to this day.

One day a neighbour came to tell us that they were selling butter at the Home and Colonial[20] and I was sent down to line up in the queue. I lined up for ages but when I got to the counter they said no children were being served. I suppose some people could send a whole family and get more than their share. One old man told them that I could have his ration, as he knew my father "who was on the big guns in France". They let us both have some. Another day they told us they were selling coal in the woodyard nearby. My brother, aged four,

and I took round a small tin bath and were sold sixpenny worth of coal. It was much better when food rationing was introduced for, although it did not allow us a great deal, we had ration books with coupons in them which entitled everyone

22 *Coldharbour Lane c1905. The Home and Colonial Store was next to the shop on the left of the road with the white awning.*

to a certain amount of butter, sugar, tea, and meat. Also, when so many young children developed rickets, small bottles of milk were served in junior schools.

The news from the Front became ever more horrifying with long lists of casualties, and the newspapers telling of horses, guns and soldiers dying in mud and sleeping and drowning in water-logged trenches.[21] But Christmas came and we had a Christmas tree. Mother made a Christmas pudding of flour, a lump of suet, which the butcher sold her above her ration, ground carrots and apples, as there was no dried fruit. We children thought it was gorgeous. As usual we three girls were told we could have a book or a doll and as usual Dorothy and I had annuals and Gladys had a black doll; my brother of course had tin soldiers.

1916 – The Telegram

Munitions were constantly in demand and quite young girls were called up to work in the munition factories. My mother wrote to the War Office to ask if my father could come home and open his workshops to make munitions. They wrote back to say my father was already doing a very necessary job but could she do with some assistance to open the workshops herself? I do not know why we did not do this. I suppose she was not that kind of person and she did have five young children to look after.

Then came the fateful day that changed our lives. The telegram came that simply said that my father had been killed. It was July 1916. I cannot remember if my mother cried. She just sat in the chair by the kitchen range holding the telegram. The baby cried and we all stood around not knowing what to do.

I knew about these telegrams. Two of my friends told me about the telegrams their parents had had when their brothers had been killed. Then Mabel Gain ushered us upstairs, with tears streaming down her face, and told us to keep quiet. The baby still cried so Mabel picked her up, and with the baby tucked underneath her arm she made a strong cup of tea for my mother and then sat down on the other side of the fire singing to the baby. I looked through the banisters and Mother was still holding the telegram. That night I heard her crying but stayed curled up very tight in bed. I was 10 years old but grew up overnight.

Life seemed to go on as it normally did. We went to school in the morning and although we had our small bottle of milk in the mornings we did not pay for it, as we were now war orphans. I think it was the Church Army or the Salvation Army that brought a large urn of hot soup along to the school and again the war orphans, of whom there were now quite a few, did not have to pay. We had our Saturday penny as usual. As the eldest I held the penny until we reached Mrs Longman's shop[22] where we spent a happy half hour deciding what to spend our farthing on. We always ended up buying the same things. I bought an inch-wide piece of liquorice from which you could tear of strips like bootlaces. Dorothy always bought dolly mixtures and Gladys bought jelly babies. Fred bought a humbug on a stick and Mrs Longman always gave us all a bag of sherbet in which you dipped a sweet on a stick and sucked it. Quite delicious!

My mother was quiet and withdrawn: no laughing and singing as she used to and she scolded us much less. The garden was her great escape and she could always be found there. She had planted nasturtiums, marigolds and hollyhocks from the seeds she had dried the autumn before. The coalman brought us our bag of coal each week, carrying the bags on a little cart drawn by a great shire horse. Often he brought a bag of stable manure and emptied it into a pit at the bottom of the garden. Mabel did such housework as got done and minded the baby, which she loved doing, wheeling the big pram round and round the garden and then to school to meet us.

To earn our Saturday penny we had to do our Saturday jobs. I ran the errands and polished the sideboard in the dining room, a large piece of furniture with a long mirror at the back. I had to stand on a chair to reach the mirror. I have never been fond of cleaning windows since. After that there were the knives to do. Some kind of red powder was sprinkled on a knifeboard and the blade of the knife was rubbed up and down on the board until all the stains were gone. There were no stainless steel knives at that time. Dorothy had to clean knives and forks. I think the same red powder was put onto a saucer and slightly damped, then rubbed onto the cutlery with a cloth and polished. Gladys polished the teaspoons. Every spring the carpets were taken up and we all banged the dust out of them with carpet-beaters. On Mondays the copper in the scullery was lighted at five o'clock in the morning for the washing I washed all the girls' black stockings in a large tub called a dolly tub, pounding them up and down with a round stick affair. I quite enjoyed that job.

We also had our pets to look after. There was a large tabby cat, answering only to "puss", who had a plate of porridge with us in the morning, and whatever he could catch during the daytime. We also had two white mice named Millicent and Marmaduke. One day poor Millicent got out and the cat chased it all the way up the stairs, followed by all the children. The cat caught the mouse, and Gladys, who was rather plump, fell down the stairs. Marmaduke would not eat and died of a broken heart.

One day a large Irish wolfhound came and sat on our front doorstep and would not go home, however much we tried. Mother gave him a plate of porridge and put a notice in one or two local shops but no one claimed him and he continued to sit on our doorstep. Eventually he was allowed into the kitchen, and had his plate of porridge when the cat had hers. He walked with us to school and on his way home he called in at the butcher's for his bone. We called him "Bindle". I am not sure why – perhaps because he was brindled in colour. When we first called him this he put his head on one side, then when we continued to call him this he came to see what we wanted, we patted him and told him he was a good dog. He always afterwards answered to the name. The main worry was how to feed such a big dog. Every morning my mother made porridge in a big black pot on the kitchen range. Then the cat had porridge, the dog had porridge, and we all had porridge without sugar, because that was rationed, and without milk which was kept for the baby. She had a rusk with hot milk poured over it and mashed up. Our porridge we had with or without salt, as we wished. My mother said that a plate of porridge and the bone that the butcher gave Bindle was not enough. He had no ration like the horses of the coalman and the milkman had, and money was getting scarce. Mabel Gain found the answer. Her friend Rosie English worked in a restaurant not far away and she often said it was scandalous, the scraps that were thrown away. Mabel took her a bowl and said she would call every evening for the scraps, which she did. Mother poured some soup on the unappetising mess and Bindle ate it with great relish. Sometimes after our afternoon walk the fire in the parlour would be lit, Bindle would lie down in front of it, and we would all put our feet on him.

Dorothy and I would practise our music on these evenings: Dorothy on a violin given to her by Miss Bruggemeyer who gave her lessons, and myself on

the piano. The Bruggemeyers, who lived over the road from us at 3 Kemerton Road were a delightful family. They were German, so Mr Bruggemeyer was interned, although he was very elderly and a retired professor from one of our own universities.[23] Mrs Bruggemeyer was a comfortable person and her two spinster daughters were very musical, one playing the piano and one the violin. They both sang beautifully. They gave Dorothy and me lessons without any charge. I was not musical but I did manage to get to "Poet and Peasant" by Franz von Suppé and loved playing the chords at the beginning. My

23 *Poet and Peasant sheet music*

naughty brother would bang on the lid of the dustbin when we practised.

1916 – Making Ends Meet

Towards the end of 1916, some weeks after my father was killed and money was getting very scarce, my mother had a letter asking her to come to London, giving her a time and a place and telling her to bring any papers to establish her husband's position before the war so that they could work out her pension. In those days the amount of pension you were paid was estimated on your husband's situation before he joined up. If he was a postman his pension was less than if he was a lawyer. My mother took the letter to the solicitor who had worked for my father. The next day he asked my mother to come and see him. Apparently, when my father had first started the business a friend of his, a certain Mr Essex, had put some money into it. When he heard that Father had been killed, he sold the workshops, the tools and the machinery, even the little car, which by now was of vintage value. He had sold his house and gone abroad with the proceeds – it was thought to Ireland. Mabel was now working at the restaurant with her friend Rosie English as my mother could no longer afford to keep her, but she still brought Bindle his evening meal and she spent her day off with us. She had no family and had come to us from an orphanage.

When my mother went to London to see about her pension there was no one to look after five children so Mother decided to take us with her. We three girls wore our Sunday white silk dresses with a black ribbon sash, my brother had on a white sailor suit with a black bow, and the baby wore a long white

24 *Coldharbour Lane between Denmark Road and Kenbury Street*

dress with a black bow on her shoulder. Babies wore long dresses until they were about six months old at that time. We were all sat on chairs once we were dressed, with dire threats as to what would happen if we moved, the baby was crying in the pram, but Mother was soon dressed herself. She wore her long black skirt with a deep frill round the bottom and which dipped slightly at the back and showed off her highly polished boots. She was always telling us that it was not important how old your shoes were so long as they were polished and shone. Her blouse was delightful. Grace Godfrey had given it to her when Vera was born. It was black, made of thick stiff silk. The sleeves were puffed at the top and fitted from the elbow down. The high neck and the front were frilled and tucked and it had small silver buttons to fasten it. She coiled her long auburn hair in a bun at the nape of her neck and tied it with a small bow at the top. Without the aid of a mirror she pinned on a little black hat with the widow's weeds hanging from the back. We all walked to Camberwell Green from where she could get a tram to London for twopence, and I suppose it was one penny for us children.[24] We all stood in a line at the kerb waiting for the tram. My mother carried baby Vera, with me on one side of her, holding fast to brother Fred, and Dorothy on the other side holding hands with Gladys. The tram rattled along the middle of the road and we all scrambled on board. The passengers made room for us. Many of the women were in tears at the sight of this young widow. Mother was only 36, with a young family and a babe in arms.

We reached London and the tram terminus and, with the kind help of the conductor, two passengers, various policemen and a doorman, we eventually reached our destination. We were in a large hall with high ceilings, a very polished floor, big windows and a large desk where a tall thin man sat. He came over to us and my mother showed him the letter. He showed us to an alcove where there were some armchairs and a table. We were so exhausted and hot we were glad to sit and look around. We wore our best Sunday black patent shoes and our feet ached. After a while a pleasant woman brought us some glasses of milk and a plate of biscuits. I particularly remember those biscuits, as they were whole ones. Biscuits were not packed as they are today but sold loose from tins. There were, of course, quite a number of broken biscuits left in the bottom of these tins, which we could buy. A large bag of broken biscuits cost only a penny.

After a while someone came for my mother. She took the baby with her, Fred and Gladys both went to sleep and Dorothy and I just sat. It seemed a long time that we sat there until someone came and took us to a canteen where my mother was waiting and we were given a meal of sausages and potatoes, followed by jelly. I cannot remember how we got home, perhaps exhaustion wiped all memory from my mind, but I know we just had bread and jam and went to bed. Apparently my mother was given the basic pension, which was not very much, until her affairs were sorted out. She went to see the solicitor and he promised to do his best for her, and she was not to worry about his fees. As my father had always said, you cannot have too many friends.

We were still very hard up so my mother decided that she had to go out to work. She found a job quite easily as a sorter in Brixton Sorting Office. Although she had to start very early in the morning she was able to get home before we were out of school. Each night our clothes for the next day were put on a chair by our bed. The black pot of porridge was on the kitchen range. I had to feed the baby with a spoon and I think she had as much in her ear as in her mouth! Dorothy and I had terrific struggles to put a clean napkin on her. Dorothy, Gladys and Fred walked round the corner to the little Church school with Bindle trotting behind them. I had to wheel the pram round to a crèche, which had been opened for the young children of war widows who had to work. It was open

25 *Brixton Sorting Office, Cornwall Road (today Blenheim Gardens)*

from 5 a.m. to 5 p.m. As I was over 10 years old I had to go to the big school in Coldharbour Lane.[25] It was quite a long walk and I was always late. I had to line up with all the naughty boys and the other latecomers for the cane. When my mother eventually heard about the cane she wrote a note and I was allowed to be 15 minutes late. The sorting office was open on Saturdays so I had to get lunch for us all. It was usually soup and sausages, but one day I made a meat pie – one which I was never allowed to forget as I put sugar in it instead of salt!

There were more and more air raids now, and one day Brixton was bombed and mother had to run all the way home through bomb damage and gunfire. The guns in Ruskin Park were really heavy and Gladys was having hysterics. She was always more upset than the rest of us.

Christmas 1916 came and the sorters had to help deliver the post on Christmas Day. We were all told to stay in bed until my mother came home. She arrived home from work about 10 a.m. We had our stockings, which had an orange, some peanuts and a bag of sweets in them. Yet again Dorothy and I had our book, Gladys had her doll and Fred some lead soldiers. The weather was very bad and the raids were getting worse.

Mother decided to change her job. She got work as an outworker for a clothing factory in Camberwell Green that mass-produced baby clothes. The pieces were cut out in blocks of a dozen and she had to sew the parts together. First the sleeves, then the bodices, the sleeves into the bodices and then the bodices into the skirts. For a dozen finished dresses you were paid the fabulous sum of one shilling and sixpence, ten shillings for six dozen. It was sweated labour and mainly done by war widows, as the women could be at home to look after their families. On Saturday afternoon the case containing the six dozen completed dresses was placed in the pram and wheeled up to the factory in Camberwell Green where they were inspected before the ten-shilling note was handed over. That evening, after Dorothy, Gladys and Fred were put to bed about eight o'clock, my mother and I would wheel the pram to Brixton Market where, by the time we arrived, they would be auctioning the meat and the fish. Not many of these stall-holders had any form of refrigeration and they liked to sell off at the end of the day all their unsold food, even if it was at give-away prices. I took care of the pram while Mother pushed her way into the crowd. You had to be quick to catch the butcher's eye when the joint you wanted was being auctioned. Eventually she would buy a joint of beef for a shilling or two. Then we went to the fish stall where, for another shilling, she got quite a packet of fish. On our way out of the market we were often given a cabbage or something that the stall-holder wanted to clear.

By the time we got home it was often after midnight but the family could be fed for another week. On Saturday mornings I would earn a few pennies running errands for an elderly lady who lived nearby. One particular errand

26 *Looking up Denmark Hill from Camberwell Green c1914*

every Saturday was for a pound of sausages from Kennedy's at Camberwell Green. She always gave me six pennies, as the sixpenny piece was small and easily lost. One Saturday I was running as usual, when I dropped two of the pennies and they rolled down a drain. I was devastated and was not sure whether to go home and ask my mother for the two pennies or to get less than a pound of sausages. Either way I would be in trouble, and possibly lose my job. I decided to go on. I went up to the butcher who always served me and told him the sorry story and asked if I could have a whole pound and bring him the two pennies the following week. When I did bring the extra money as promised, he laughed and told me to go and buy myself some sweets. I have never forgotten his kindness.

1917 – The Vicar Calls – Paulerspury

It was soon after this that the Vicar came round to see us to tell us that a fund called the Country Holiday scheme had been organised to take war orphans

27 St Saviour's parish magazine cover

who were living in areas vulnerable to air raids for a holiday away to quiet country areas. Country people who volunteered to take children were paid to look after them and feed them well. The Vicar said he thought that Grace was looking pale and thin and needed a holiday. My mother said "She is always pale and thin but is perfectly well and strong". The Revd Bayfield Clark was tall and well fed, and was very fond of laying down the law. His large vicarage was beautifully furnished and he drove around in a carriage and pair, which shone with much polishing by a coachman who was also the gardener and odd job man. The Revd Bayfield Clark was married to the daughter of the Bishop of London, a stately and severe-looking person.[26]

The Revd Bayfield Clark looked round the room with its comfortable chairs, the well-polished piano and the shelves of books, and suggested that my mother could sell her piano as she was now a widow and must need the money with five children to look after. My highly emotional mother was standing by a table with a vase of flowers on it and for a moment I thought he was going to get that vase of flowers right in the middle of his well-filled embroidered waistcoat! She was quite capable of doing so but instead said quite quietly, in her best up-country voice, laced with overtones of acid, that we managed very well with the small amount of money a grateful country allowed her, and what she earned through sweated labour. You could not embarrass the man, he was too sure of his own importance! He admired the flowers and then suggested that Dorothy and I should go with this Country Holiday scheme for two weeks in the Easter holidays.

It was later arranged that we would go to Paulerspury, a little village in

Northamptonshire a few miles from Towcester. Off we went with much
excitement, but a little frightened. We had never been away from home before.
We were billeted with a pleasant country woman in a cottage next to a farm. We
had farm eggs, milk and butter and Mrs Watson made her own bread and cakes,
and such delicacies as jelly and trifle. I expect we would have grown fat had we
been there longer. The war seemed a long way away, except for the shortage
of young men, the farms being looked after by the women and girls. Wages
were paid by the Government to girls that were not in the war or the munition
factories.

The Vicar was a kindly old man who had been brought out of retirement as
the young vicar had gone as a chaplain to the forces. The old man came to see
us and brought us some apples from his store. Soon the two weeks were up and
Dorothy and I were happy to be back in London with the family and Bindle,
who gave us a lovely wet kiss with his long tongue. We chatted for forever until
we were told to shut up and stop showing off! We then had to get used, again,
to air raids and guns and porridge, to half an egg on Sunday morning and
sharing a bed.

THE GREEN, PAULERSPURY.

28 Paulerspury c1918

One evening Jack rode round on his bicycle shouting "Take cover". The
anti-aircraft guns started firing in Ruskin Park, Gladys began screaming, we
gathered in the kitchen round the range sitting on the floor as usual, when a
bomb fell on the park. I suppose the German pilot had been trying to hit the

gun emplacement but it fell at the farther end of the park and although there seemed to be no damage to the house the china fell off the dresser and the saucepans off the fire.[27] Bindle and Puss ran under the kitchen table which was always there as a refuge in troubled times. Dorothy, Fred and I went with them, Gladys and the baby both screaming. There was pandemonium. My mother swept up the bits of china and put it all in a bucket, pushed Gladys under the table with us and mopped up the water spilled from the kettle. I am not sure that she really knew what she was saying but she told us that we would go away to the country in the morning, that we would "go to Paulerspury to stay".

The next morning we were all packed up, washed and excited, and I think my mother too wanted a change. How we managed to arrive in Towcester I cannot imagine, but I do remember walking down the street wondering how far it was to Paulerspury. We must have made a strange little group; Mother pushing the pram with the suitcase she normally used to carry the baby dresses to the factory, and each or us carrying our own bundle. We had our Sunday dress and shoes, a change of' clothes, stockings and another gingham dress. Bindle trotted behind. It was July and very hot. The little town was very busy. Farm horses plodded along the road pulling their carts full of noisy pigs and sheep kept in with big nets. Now and then a beautifully groomed horse trotted along pulling a smart buggy with highly polished brass lamp-holders and driven by capable-looking women in tweed jackets. There were plenty of bicycles and the occasional car. Young women in brown overalls, probably from a nearby munitions factory, hurried past, and other women with their shopping baskets sometimes looked curiously at the little group now walking wearily along the hot pavement. Then a shout of "Whoa!" startled us and a great shire horse drew up at the roadside. The feathers around his feet were well brushed and shining and his eyes were blinkered against the flies. The brasses on his harness shone in the sun. He was well cared for. An elderly man was in the driving seat of an open-topped farm cart. His face was lined and weather beaten but his eyes twinkled as he gazed at our anxious faces. A wide-brimmed felt hat covered his grey hair which grew down almost to his shoulders. His jacket hung loosely on thin shoulders. It had probably fitted him when he was a young man. He looked at the young woman in black – the little round hat was now slightly askew and the mass of bright auburn hair was threatening to tumble down her back at any moment. "You a widow woman?" he asked. "Yes," said my mother, "my husband was killed last summer and I am trying to take the children away from the bombing for a while. Can you tell me how far it is to Paulerspury?" "I am going there. I will take you." He climbed down and opened up the back of the cart. We clambered in joyfully and the driver helped my mother push the pram into the middle of the cart. There were bench seats on either side. Freddie sat on Mother's lap and was soon asleep, Dorothy sat close by her side and Gladys and I sat on the other side. Bindle trotted along beside Nobby the horse. We trundled lazily along leafy lanes, with the sun shining down on us making us drowsily comfortable after our exhausting morning. Bindle stopped to sniff at the verges here and there and then easily caught up with Nobby's slow and steady pace. Our elderly benefactor smoked his pipe and was silent. It was very peaceful.

We arrived at Paulerspury and Nobby stopped at the gates of the vicarage. "Have to see the vicar," said our elderly driver as he climbed down and let down the back of the cart. "I take his eggs and fruit into the market, could give you a lift any time, get here at eight in the morning and back about now". He helped my mother with the pram and we all clambered out clutching our little bundles. Mother wanted to pay him, but he would have none of it, waving us goodbye he trudged off up the vicarage drive. We stood and looked around. There was the village green that we remembered and the shop with its straggle of cottages. Dorothy and I led the way to the little house that we had stayed at earlier in the year at Easter time. It was a little newer than most of the cottages. My mother put on her very resolute face and knocked at the door. It had a dull echoing and unfriendly sound and we were apprehensive. I looked through the window. The house was empty. We sat on the steps and considered our position. We all agreed that it was not possible to go all that way home that night so it meant staying somewhere for the night and going home tomorrow. We were all getting hungry and the baby was crying. I sat on the grass with Bindle and foraged among the blankets for a bottle of milk which I knew I had put there with a packet of Farley's rusks. Baby Vera could drink from a cup now but it was easier with a bottle as she could hold it herself. The packet of rusks I shared amongst us all, even Bindle. He ate his in two bites and a swallow, then looked enviously at Vera's but did not touch it. We all felt better; the rusks had taken the edge off our hunger.

Gladys and Fred had an argument, which ended in a fight as usual. I suggested we all went round the back to see if there was a window that we could open. All the windows were tight shut but there was an outhouse that had no door on it. It was quite large and had a copper in one corner and an old table with some sacks on it. At least we could put the sacks on the floor and sleep there for the night, and possibly get some bread from the village shop in the morning. We brought our tired mother round to see our discovery. We were all exhausted but Mother cried and went back again to sit on the steps. I think she was now regretting that she had listened to us and gone on this hare-brained adventure. Vera had crawled down the lane followed by Bindle. I brought her back and shut the gate, but then she crawled determinedly to the flower bed and started to eat the marigolds. She was probably hungry but I did not think that marigolds were the answer, even if the gypsies do put them in their diet! I strapped her in her pram and shoved a rattle at her, so she screamed. We did not take any notice, as we never did. She always shut up after a while.

A pleasant-faced woman came out of the farmhouse next door and walked over to see what all the noise was about. She leaned over the gate, recognising Dorothy and me at once as the two little girls who came to the farm for milk and eggs during the Easter holidays. Of course we all started talking at once, Mother trying to get her word in as well, until Mrs Smith, for that was her name, said "Be quiet and let your mother speak". Mother told her our sorry tale and asked her if she knew of anyone who could put us up for the night and possibly provide us with a meal as the children were all very hungry. Mrs Smith looked at us thoughtfully, at my mother, tired and white-faced, then at the baby who was watching her with some interest and at the children with their grubby dresses and dirt-streaked faces. But she was a brave woman as well as a kindly one. "My two sons are in France and their rooms are empty and doing nothing," she said. "Come along and we will find some tea for you." We washed our faces and hands at the pump in the yard and changed into clean dresses. Then we trooped shyly into a large, bright farmhouse kitchen. The floor was of grey flagstones with a big rag rug in front of a kitchen range. The range was set in a brick alcove, almost like a small room with a bench on either side. Above the range in the chimney a ham hung on a hook, and a great black kettle stood on top of the range hissing quietly.

We had never had such a tea. There were thick slices of home-cured bacon, and lovely fried eggs and glistening fried tomatoes. Mrs Smith cut thick slices of home-made bread spread with farmhouse butter and home-made plum jam. We had mugs of warm milk while Mother and Mrs Smith drank innumerable cups of tea from a brown teapot. We made quite a big tea party round the table that evening as Mrs Smith had two boys from Dr Barnardo's staying with her. John, the older one, was a tall, strong lad of about 14 with an intelligent face and a shock of fair hair. He helped Mrs Smith on the farm. He had left the school at Dr Barnardo's but worked in the evening on papers which were sent to him, as he was hoping to pass the entrance examination for Dartmouth College to train as a naval officer. The other boy was younger, about eight years old; he was only staying at the farm for the holidays. He was a thin nervous-faced little chap. "He is called Stinker," said Mrs Smith. "He wets his bed and sometimes his trousers but he will be all right with plenty of good food. His mother ran away and left him with a bully of a father who is now in prison for theft. That's why he is now at Dr Barnardo's."

Bindle was gnawing at a bone in the scullery which led off from the kitchen and which had in it the inevitable copper and a stone sink with a pump. "Now wench," said Mrs Smith, when we were all happily quiet, "John and I have to go on an errand in the village." She put the bread and jam away. "The girls can wash up. You have a sit by the fire, we shall not be long."

John looked surprised but got up and followed her out. Mother sat in a chair by the fire nursing the baby. I imagine she was exhausted, as much from anxiety as anything else. Gladys and Fred sat on a rug with Bindle between them. They were not arguing or fighting, for once. That left Dorothy and me to do the washing up. We pumped some water into the big yellow sink and poured hot water from the kettle and just piled the dishes into it. I washed up and Dorothy dried and we both felt very capable.

Presently Mrs Smith and John came back pulling a hand-cart with a cot and a small iron bedstead in it. "Now wench," she said as she came in – she always called my mother "wench", which seemed to me to be nice and friendly – "come up and see where you sleep." We all budged up the stairs, John and Stinker and Bindle came as well. I imagine we were probably a diversion in the routine of their lives. There was a pleasant room, plainly furnished with a double bed and a small iron bedstead which we three girls could have, and a similar room with the cot that Mother, Freddie and the baby could use. "The two boys have a room at the end of the passage and John looks after Stinker so they won't bother you. I sleep the other end of the house and when I get to bed I don't wake till cockcrow, so don't let anything bother you."

The next morning when we came down at about seven both Mrs Smith and John had gone out. Stinker was sitting on the rug in front of the fire with Bindle. We girls washed our faces and hands as quickly as possibly and Freddie was forcibly washed, with much yelling. Stinker told us where to find the porridge oats and Mother bathed the baby while the porridge was cooking. There was plenty of milk and we all enjoyed our breakfast, Stinker as well.

When we had cleared away Mother scrubbed the kitchen table and then she got down on her hands and knees and scrubbed the floor with the baby's bath water. We found a box of brushes at the bottom of a cupboard, so Mother polished the kitchen range with black polish while I cleaned the steel fender with a piece of emery paper. Mother was not fond of housework but she liked the after-effect, so she did it. It was a good thing that she had an old skirt and shirt in case.

Our two little ginghams were always in the wash until Mother had a brilliant idea. Where clothes were concerned she was a genius, keeping us well dressed on next to nothing. She asked Mrs Smith for some flour sacks. Then they were well scrubbed and put out into the sun to dry. A hole was cut out of the bottom shaped for our heads to go through. The sides were slit for armholes and a belt tied round the middle. We loved them and they cost nothing and kept our dresses for smart wear, like Sunday School, which the Vicar and Mother insisted on. John pleaded work – and Stinker was always missing.

One day Mrs Smith said she had to take the pig to market in the morning and asked John to scrub her. She was a huge fat sow with about 15 piglets and very muddy. I helped John pour a bucket of soapy water on her. I think she enjoyed that as it was now August and still very hot. Then we scrubbed her with stiff brooms while she grunted and wagged that silly little tail. Then we cleaned her sty and put a lot of straw down so that she wouldn't be too dusty in the morning.

In the morning the sow and all her piglets were put into a cart and a net fastened down over them. Before Mrs Smith and John went off she asked my mother if she would stay around the house until she got back as she kept her money under the mattress on her bed. Apparently Mrs Smith had heard that the Germans were getting short of money. She would not trust the banks at the moment, because if the Germans came they would take over the banks and her money would be confiscated. She also said she didn't trust Stinker all that much. This worried my mother so much that she sat on the bed all day and I had to get the dinner.

We had forgotten about Germans as the war seemed so far away. When my father was killed, Vickers sent her some money which she had put in the bank, and every pound she had managed to scrape together had also gone into the bank as she knew the Germans would not pay her a pension. We discussed this at length while we sat on the bed and came to the conclusion that money under the mattress was not on either, as she or I would be sitting on the bed all day. The bank manager was another friend of my father's so we decided to ask him. I was 11 but my poor mother had no one else to consult now, so I did my best, though I was not the most practical of persons. I myself had a red tin money box that had a halfpenny in it. My Saturday piano pennies always seemed to get spent in Brixton market.

Mrs Smith arrived home about teatime very pleased with the price she had got for her breeding pig and the piglets. She had bought some new young hens and some chicks which delighted us. We had boiled eggs for tea and an enormous amount of bread and jam, while we listened to the market gossip. Nothing could be further from our thoughts than the war and Germans.

The next day John asked Dorothy and me if we would like to earn some money. Apparently Thomas Tickler was paying a penny a bucket for fallen apples to make jam for the Army. The vicar said his orchard was full of fallen apples and we were welcome to come and pick them up. John scrubbed some farm buckets and he took two and Dorothy and I took one each. There was a large tent in the vicar's drive arid two young women sat at a table and took our names. We soon filled our buckets with fallen apples. Only the apples without maggots were wanted, and of course there were a great many half-eaten by wasps and maggots which we swept up in a pile for the vicar's compost heap. John filled his buckets twice over but I had to help Dorothy as she was frightened by wasps. We took our buckets along to the tent where the apples were tipped out into big skips. In the evening a lorry came and took them away. We arrived home at teatime tired, dusty and hungry but happily clutching our pennies. John had to do his chores on the farm in the mornings and we had to help in the house, but each afternoon we went down to pick up the fallen apples and John climbed trees to pick plums and damsons. There were not so many apples now, but they were easier as they were not so full of maggots and wasps. In September we were given smaller enamel buckets and we went around the fields and down the lanes picking blackberries. It took longer to fill our buckets but we still only got penny for a bucket but we enjoyed ourselves. It was just as well that we had our sacking overalls as our little gingham dresses would never have survived the stains and scratches.

I put my pennies away in the little red money box and carefully placed it under the bed. I thought it might be a little uncomfortable under the mattress. Then John discovered a lovely way to save money quite safely. We went to the Post Office in the general shop in the village. The postmistress gave us a form with space for our names and addresses and 12 spaces for penny stamps. When we had 12 stamps on our form we took it to the Post Office and were given a little Post Office book in which she wrote the date and an entry of one shilling. I was extremely proud of this little book and took it out every evening and gloated over it, like a miser. By the end of September I had four shillings entered, but strangely enough I have no idea what happened to my four shillings or the little savings book.

1917-18 – My Salvation, Andrew Carnegie

The end of September came and the holidays were over and we had to go back to school. Someone from Barnardo's came for Stinker. He and Gladys were much the same age and got along quite well together. The little boy was looking much fatter and no longer wet his trousers but I was not so sure about the bed wetting. We still called the poor little chap Stinker. John had another two years of working on the farm before he was 16 and could sit for his entrance exam for Dartmouth College. I was sure he would be accepted as he was strong, intelligent and trustworthy, and quite a leader.

We helped to pack our little bundles and Mrs Smith packed the corners of the pram with butter and eggs and jars of jam and a home-made loaf of bread. Puss was sitting on the doorstep when we arrived home. She looked fat and well cared for and apparently pleased to see us. The sun was shining which helped dispel the gloom of a house that had not been lived in for two months. The breakfast things were still on the kitchen table and the cups still had tea in them. The bucket of broken china was standing by the garden door. In fact it was just as we had left it in such a hurry two months before. We cleared up and lit the kitchen range. The one thing we had plenty of was fuel, as kind Mrs Bruggemeyer had told the coalman to shoot our weekly sack of coal down into the cellar and he would be paid when we got home. There was a grating by the front steps, which could be lifted, and the coal shot into the cellar.

Life soon settled down to normal and Bindle resumed his escort duties to school and his visits to the butcher's. We had to get used to the war again, to the guns and air raids and soldiers, but somehow we were now terribly used to the news of dreadful casualties both to men and women at the front and to civilians at home. We did not take a newspaper now but when the air raids seemed to be near we were all brought down to the kitchen until the "all clear" went. Our mother being at home made a great deal of difference to us.

My salvation was Andrew Carnegie and his libraries. There was one at the top of a lane near to us called Red Post Hill. It was a rough, uphill country lane with fields around it and the library at the top.[28] The librarian was very good to us, and because we could only take home one book at a time she allowed us to sit and read one book there and then take one home. After a while I had read all the books suitable for my age and all the children's classics, so I was allowed to have a book from the adult library provided the librarian vetted my choice or suggested one herself.

I read all Baroness Orczy books and quite a number of Dickens. Reading at this time was my great escape and joy. Whenever possible, my real pleasure was to pick some apples off the tree and find a corner to hide and read. Often I was in trouble because no one could find me when I was wanted to run an errand

29 Carnegie Library on Herne Hill Road c1914, before development reached the top of the hill

or mind the baby. One day my mother got in a temper with me and threw my book on the fire. It was a library book and had to be replaced.

Then it was Christmas 1917 and more big parties for war orphans, with Father Christmas and Christmas trees. We only went to one of these as we found children en masse rather terrifying.

The Revd Bayfield Clark came to see us and told me that I would have to go to classes one evening a week as I was to be confirmed at Easter. His wife's father, the Bishop of London,[29] was coming to confirm us. I had to learn the Ten Commandments, the Lord's Prayer, the Catechism, the Creed and, it seemed, more or less the whole of the morning service. There were about 12 of us boys and girls, and we had to work hard to get word perfect in two months. For the confirmation service I had a new white silk dress and a white veil with a cross embroidered on the front and Grace Godfrey gave me a prayer book with a white cover. I had never seen anyone so awe-inspiring as the Bishop of London in his ceremonial robes.

Although we had promised with tearful goodbyes to come back again to Paulerspury the next summer, we never did. My mother always had wanderlust those days. Sometimes, when we had upset her, she would put Vera, who was now getting to be a big girl and could walk quite well, in the pram and go off all day. When she did this Bindle would sit on the doorstep until she came home. Sometimes it would be late in the evening and she never said where she had been.

The solicitor had managed to get her the pension she was entitled to and they also paid her the arrears. She no longer had to make the baby dresses but made all our clothes and we still went to Brixton market on Saturday evenings.

As the evenings became brighter it seemed the air raids got worse and the guns in Ruskin Park louder.[30] There were young men around now, some on crutches and some with empty sleeves. Young nurses pushed others around in wheelchairs.[31]

When the summer holidays came we went again to the country, but this time my mother had rented a cottage in Essex near Thaxted. It was a pleasant little town with an old market square and architecturally interesting buildings

30 *Thaxted, Town Street c1920*

and quite a famous church beautifully maintained. The cottage was an ancient gem, quite a walk from the town on a lane leading down to a river with a mill. The front door opened into the main living room. Evidently someone came to clean the cottage for each new tenant, because the flagstone floor was scrubbed and polished. There was a rug before a recessed fireplace which burned logs, as the cupboard at the side was stacked with them. An armchair stood on either side of the fireplace and there was a couch along the wall under a small window, in the middle of the room was a well-scrubbed table with four kitchen chairs. We were most excited to see on the middle of the table a basket with a loaf of bread, some butter and eggs and some honey, no note or bill or anything at all to say who put them there. Also on the table was an oil lamp with a tall glass shade. Leading out of this room was a scullery in which stood an old gas stove with some cooking pots and a box of matches. The copper was in the corner with a sink and pump. There was no electricity, and only water from the well. Outside in a cobbled yard there was a trough with a pump. In the two months we were there we learned to live. Now we were running around discovering things like the blue china in a cupboard and candles in a drawer. A short flight of oak stairs went up to two small bedrooms with two single beds, a chair and a chest of drawers in each. There were hooks on the back of the doors that led from one room to another and the floorboards ran slightly uphill so that you were always sliding down to the bottom of the bed. My mother, Freddie and Vera had one room and Dorothy and Gladys had the other. I slept on the couch downstairs. I quite liked this arrangement as my mother left me a nightlight when she turned the lamp out and after everyone had gone to bed Bindle would creep in from the scullery and sleep next to the couch.

There was no shop nearby but a van came round once a week with vegetables and fish, but for anything else we walked to Thaxted. Bindle came with us and sat outside the butcher's shop. We explained about the bone he used to collect on his way home from school and the butcher sold us a large bag of bones for a penny or two. My mother made some stock from these and then gave them to Bindle. He missed his evening meal of scraps and had to have porridge as we often did.

On Fridays, before tea, we were sent down to the river with a towel and a bag of yellow soap where we washed and splashed each other near to the bank. Vera was bathed in the copper on wash-day.

We enjoyed our holiday. Most days we went out exploring the countryside, taking a packed lunch, arriving home tired and hungry, and going to bed soon after our evening meal.

Then it was time to go back to school again and to guns and raids, although there were not quite so many raids and apparently the Germans were not winning the war – although more of our school friends had lost brothers and fathers and many of them wore black sashes or bows.

1918 – The War is Over

Then it seemed quite suddenly the war was over and the country went crazy. There were parties everywhere and in many places whole streets celebrated with tables all down the road and people cooking whatever they had. Even pianos were brought out, and everyone was singing and dancing. We were taken to see them and people tried hard to make us join in, but my mother was very quiet and spent most of her time in the garden.

We went to school as usual, and the headmistress, Miss Warner, was very kind to us. She had liked my father and did her best to help by taking my rather naughty brother into her own class when the young mistress in the juniors couldn't cope. At playtime we could often hear the children chanting "Army on Freddie Lucas".[32] He and his only friend, a young black boy, often wrought havoc until the cane was brought into play, wielded by the P.E. mistress, Miss

31 *Street celebration November 1918, Oakbank Grove Herne Hill*

Ross. Actually Freddie was a clever and good-looking little boy. He was reading at six years old but sisters surrounded him and his mother had a new baby girl. He needed a father.

Professor Bruggemeyer came home. His hair was very white and he was very thin, but he quietly went back to his reading and writing as if nothing had happened.[33] I only saw him when I went to my piano lesson with Miss Bruggemeyer, but he was always pleasant and courteous, and would smile and say how much he had enjoyed my music.

Gradually the men came back from the front – those that had jobs to go back to were lucky. Where there had been long queues at the drill halls to volunteer for Kitchener's Army there were now even longer queues at the employment exchanges. The men brought many illnesses back from the trenches, among them a particularly nasty virus, which for some reason was called Spanish 'flu. Many thousandsof people died from it, especially young children and the elderly. I caught it, and Dr Cooper[34] got quite worried and came almost every day to see me. There were three things I particularly remember about this illness. There was the hot-water-bottle wrapped in a towel which I hugged all day, and the screen which was put round the bed to keep the draughts out. It was a large four-panelled screen covered in a brown hessian or canvas and we children were each given a panel to stick scraps on, flowers and birds and animals – in fact anything that took our fancy. It was always put around our bed if any of us were sick, as our bedrooms had no heating. The third thing I remember was the day Auntie Lil came to see the invalid. I had my eyes shut as I suppose I did not feel like talking. I remember her saying, "I hope you've got her insured, Charlotte, I don't think she is going to live". From that day I was determined to get better. I did of course get better. Meanwhile, Gladys grew to my height and then passed me. My hair fell out in handfuls. My mother went to the chemist's, and they suggested a hair tonic called Bay Rum and Cantharides[35] which she rubbed in every night. It grew back quite thick and bushy, but I lost my dark chestnut hair which went well with my eyes – I thought they were hazel but was always told they were green. My mother called my new mop of hair light brown but everyone else called it mousey.

The doctor thought that sea air would be good for me, so when the summer came we went for two weeks to Margate. The two weeks by the sea cost more than two months in the country in the previous two years, but we children thought it was marvellous. Rosie English came with us to help my mother, and the owner of the guest house cooked us breakfast and an evening meal. Mabel Gain had married a young soldier, a pleasant North Country lad, and he had gone back to his work on a big estate in Yorkshire where he and Mabel had a tied cottage. She was so happy that she looked quite pretty. Rosie had come to us on her days off, brought Bindle his supper of scraps and helped my mother wherever she could. Her main job on this seaside holiday seemed to be counting heads in the sea. Bindle had been left with the Bruggemeyers, who were very fond of him.

Although we enjoyed our holiday by the sea it was soon over and we spent the rest of the school holidays in the garden or sitting on the garden wall watching the soldiers "cleaning up" the park after the guns had gone. Turves were laid on the bare patches and the area was taped off so the boys couldn't play cricket for some time, but the hut that had housed the gun crews was painted up and made into a cricket pavilion.

Christmas 1918 was a quiet but quite a happy one. Since I was confirmed I was expected to go to church on Sunday mornings instead of Sunday school, and the Revd Bayfield Clark expected us to go on Christmas morning. I went by myself, wearing my new winter Sunday dress, a velvet one. My mother had embroidered a chrysanthemum on the front. I always remember that dress, especially as everyone in church said how pretty it was.

Rosie English came to us that Christmas. She was there when I got home and we set the table in the dining room instead of the kitchen. The kitchen was warmer, but the fire was lighted and we had candles on the table and Rosie made paper hats, which was fun.

After dinner we went into the parlour and played games: Ludo and Snakes & Ladders. We played games such as "Beat your Neighbour Out of Doors" and "Old Maid",[36] but we gave that up when Gladys kept being the Old Maid and wept bitterly. We also had active games such as "The Farmer Wants a Wife". Even Bindle joined in when we got to "we all pat the dog".[37] Very exciting. Of course Dorothy and I had to do our piano and violin duet and I had to play my "Poet and Peasant".

We had our usual complimentary tickets for the Drury Lane pantomime and on the day after Boxing Day Dorothy, Gladys and I went up to London with Mother, while Rosie English gallantly minded Freddie and Vera. The

32 *Florence Smithson as Cinderella*

pantomime was *Cinderella* that year[38] and we were transported out of this world. We laughed at the clowns, booed the ugly sisters and cheered the cats and mice who became coachmen and footmen, and we loved the fairy godmother. When Cinderella couldn't get to the ball we wept for her, and when she did go to the ball and was nearly late getting away we held our breath until she headed home again. The beautiful coach was drawn by two small white ponies.

For weeks afterwards, Dorothy and I wrote plays which were part-pantomime, part-fantasy and wholly stupendous. We were fortunate in our dressing-up clothes. The warehouse where Fred Karno had stored his theatrical clothes for his dancing girls and musical shows had caught fire, and the dresses that were not utterly destroyed were spoiled by water, so he gave them to us for dressing-up clothes.

Our dressing room was under the big table with the green cloth pulled down for a curtain. Our poor mother clapped and applauded our efforts and was then revived with copious cups of tea from her precious store. We did, however, enjoy ourselves without much expense.

1919 – An Unexpected Holiday

In the spring of 1919 the question of our education arose and I remember some very charming and efficient-looking men came to interview us. It was decided that we three girls should go to James Allen's Girls' School in Dulwich. We went to the school to sit our entrance exam just before Easter and I believe we did quite well. It was not really surprising, as we had received excellent teaching at the little church school of St Saviour's round the corner. The mistresses at St Saviour's Middle Class School for Girls and Infants were dedicated maiden ladies from good families. Most teachers were unmarried and their families had to pay the fees for their training, therefore they were mainly from middle-class families. The headmistress was Miss Warner, a delightful person who was a great help in advising my mother. The senior mistress was a Miss Maulley, a very elegant lady who floated around in long velvet dresses and was responsible for our deportment, our good manners and our English and French for the 10-year-olds. It was a great disgrace if you could not read by the time you were six years old. Miss Ross, a mannish type with ginger hair, a tweed suits and sensible shoes, taught P.E. It was mainly running and jumping in the playground – and swimming, cold water of course. She also taught Arithmetic, done the hard way with no calculators. Very few of the pupils went to their senior school without being able to read, write and cope with the essentials in Arithmetic. We had a great big globe in Geography lessons, and we all learned where the countries of the world were. We also had Country Dancing lessons and Drawing. In fact, a good basic training by good teachers who were genuinely concerned. We were accepted to go to JAGS in the following September. I understand the fees were paid for by my father's regiment.

That summer at the beginning of the school holiday, a regular Army officer, a Captain Corbett-Winder who knew my

33 *Old postcard view of Vaynor Park, Berriew, Montgomeryshire*

father,[39] came to visit us and suggested that I go to his father's estate in Wales. It was a mile from the village of Berriew, called Vaynor.[40] He said he was

34 Bridge over the River Rhiw, Berriew (photo 2018)

picking up his two girls from school in London, St Paul's School, I think, and would meet me at Paddington Station.

We travelled in a first-class carriage, most comfortably. Captain Corbett-Winder gave me a little magazine to read then sat in a corner and disappeared behind *The Times*. I think he went to sleep. His two daughters, Millicent and Lettice,[41] sat in the opposite corner. After being introduced and saying hello they talked to each other and ignored me entirely. Quite possibly they were as shy of me as I was of them. I was quite content to sit and watch the passing scenery. I was better-looking than they were, which, although rather catty, made me happy.

Vaynor Park was beautiful, with great trees and sweeping lawns. There were wooded hills and a tumbling river. I didn't see much of the girls, but their brother John was quite different and we spent many happy days riding their two little Welsh ponies bareback, fishing in the river and going on long walks. He was good company and, I think, glad to have someone who enjoyed an active life out of doors.

35 The Corbett-Winder family, c1921 (John Lyon, in the centre, his father on the right and his mother behind him)

In later years, John became Lord Lieutenant of Montgomeryshire. Captain Corbett-Winder went back to London after a few days but his father, Brigadier

36 *Lady Powis,*
  by John Singer Sargent (1912)

Corbett-Winder,[42] was very kind, if a trifle vague. He always called me Kate and never quite knew who I was, but I answered to Kate – in fact, I quite liked the name. He was a keen ornithologist and would often take John and me on long walks, stopping now and again to use his binoculars and telling us about the various birds that we saw. He also grew Parma violets for the market. He grew them under glass frames, right along one wall. I remember their wonderful scent when they were watered in the evening.

Mrs Corbett-Winder liked walking, and she would walk down the long drive to the village with a rucksack on her back to do the shopping. John and I would go with her and after the shopping she took us to the inn – the Green Dragon,[43] where we sat on a bench with a glass of lemonade and she would sit on a high stool by the bar and gossip with the locals. So she kept in touch with all that went on in the village.

Lady Powis came to stay for a long weekend during the summer.[44] She came in her caravan, which was quite a delight. Apparently she was a member of the Caravan Club, a prestigious club at that time. It wasn't much larger than a gypsy caravan and was drawn by two large horses. A large tent could be hooked on the outside for her maid and the coachman, her husband.

At the beginning of October my mother received a letter requesting her to go to Woolwich Barracks to receive my father's medals on the ninth of the

37 *St George's Garrison Church, Woolwich c1910*

month. She asked Rosie English if she would look after the younger children, and I went with her. We had new red coats and white berets, which was most exciting. My mother still wore black although it was three years since my father had been killed. The lovely blouse Grace Godfrey had given her came out of its tissue paper; also her long black skirt and the same little round hat. She wore

38 *Fred Lucas's medals, awarded for service in the Second Boer War and First World War*

that lovely auburn knot of hair in a kind of a fine net called, I think, a chignon.

We were late, of course, having some difficulty in finding the place. Instead of being among the first of a number of men and women to receive the medals,[45] she was the last. The slim elegant figure looked very lonely crossing the great barrack square lined with soldiers. After the ceremony there was a memorial service in St George's Garrison Church.[46] The church was filled with Army men and the singing was beautiful. The trumpeters were in a gallery at the back of the church, and when they sounded "The Last Post" I cried. It was so beautiful, final and lonely.

1920 – Hopes are Dashed

I had started at our new school. Dorothy and I went first and Gladys was to go the following year and, in the meantime, stay at St Saviour's. I quite enjoyed the work and made a few friends. I am not so sure about Dorothy. She wrote beautiful essays and stories but always found spelling difficult. I used to help her with her work in the evenings.

When I was 14 I was entered for an Art scholarship to Southampton Row Art College in London. We were expected to consider our careers at a much earlier age than young people are today. I had to submit a comprehensive number of subjects, and in addition to my usual schoolwork it took me over a year. I needed a portfolio of drawings and designs. Two afternoon teacloths with the hems embroidered with Richelieu embroidery, of my own design, and one with drawn threadwork; also two garments – one, a nightdress with 80 hand-sewn graduated tucks, and one of my own choice, hand-sewn and embroidered. Also a subject chosen by my Art mistress. She asked me to embroider a fine screen. I designed and embroidered a grapevine; I expect I cheated a little, as there was a picture of a grapevine on the wall of the Carnegie. I embroidered it on a fine canvas with bunches of grapes and tendrils and, I hoped, the correct leaves, as I had never seen a grapevine. It was put into a wooden frame and I was most proud of it. I embroidered one tablecloth with a Richelieu edge about six inches deep and one with a drawn threadwork edge – and I was heartily sick of them both when they were finished as they took me ages to do!

For the garment of my own choice, the Art mistress was appalled when I asked for some black cotton material. I wanted something different from a dress or a pinafore, both suggested to me, so I made an artist's smock and embroidered the bodice with smocking in red. It had full sleeves smocked at the wrists and I embroidered a palette and paintbrush on a big pocket in case the judges did not know what it was. It was much admired by my school friends. The nightdress was a nightmare to do, with 80 graduated tucks, and I left it to last.

The scholarship was open to young people aged 14 to 16 and I expect there were quite a number of entrants, so I was wildly elated when I heard I had been given the scholarship. The college sent me a form, which, among other things, asked me to pick the subject I wished to specialise in. Included in the list was dress designing, which both the Art mistress and I thought would be most interesting and useful for me.

My mother became very emotional about it and said she could not see how studying Art in any form was going to earn me a living and she could not bear the thought of my becoming a little dressmaker working all hours of the day and night for a few shillings. No explaining made any difference and we were all in the doghouse – the school, the Art mistress and myself. In the end she went to see Miss Warner, the headmistress of our little church school, who had advised her so often before. My mother told her she wanted me to go into a shop or an office to earn much-needed money.

I was asked if I would like to train as a teacher. I thought of all my teachers and decided that it was not for me. Miss Warner then suggested I should go to St George's College in Red Lion Square in central London to train for a Civil Service exam and would then be sure of a well-paid job. This was thought to be a good idea and I was not consulted further. The Art College was informed that I was unable to accept the scholarship and I imagine they gave it to the next best applicant.

1921-22 – St George's College

St George's College accepted me and my father's regiment agreed to pay the fees. I started there in September and was the youngest student and always immensely shy of all the tall and clever-looking girls there. In spite of my disappointment in not going to Art College I was quite happy at St George's, although the work was very demanding. The mistresses were all university grad-uates, some of them MAs, which was unusual for women in those days.

The English mistress, Miss Tennant, I liked very much. She was most kind to me and helped me enormously with my essays, which she said were very imaginative and unusual but needed some polishing. The headmistress was

39 *William Braginton*

Miss Braginton, whose brother was Master of King's College London.[47] Miss Braginton apparently showed him some of my essays and he asked to see me. I was very scared but he was a kindly, elderly man who talked to me about authors, most of whom I had never heard of, and suggested that I should work hard for entrance to London University to read English. When I spoke of this to my mother she was horrified and said it was necessary that I earned a living as soon as possible.

After a while the daily journey became very tiring. I had to be at St George's by a quarter to nine, which meant leaving home very early to travel by tram to London and then walk from the terminus to Red Lion Square, arriving in a lady-like manner with my hat on straight and my gloves on. I would arrive home in the evening tired and hungry and, after a meal, would work on the preparation of lessons for the next day until bedtime. Often, I helped Dorothy with her French and her spelling. She wrote very well but was hopeless at spelling.

It was decided that I should stay with my Auntie Belle, who had a restaurant in Shoe Lane off Fleet Street. My aunt was, of course, called Isabelle, after her French mother.[48] She was a tall, good-looking woman with dark hair and eyes, and was very vivacious. Although she had five children of her own she was quite happy to fit me in. Her two elder sons, George and Frank, were apprenticed to another branch of the Lucas family who had an engineering works in the Midlands. Her third son, Ernie, who was three years older than me, was musical, eccentric, fun, and took me under his wing – when he remembered. He had a baby grand piano in the restaurant and, when he was not employed in the restaurant, played and composed music. He took me to a promenade concert at the Albert Hall and then forgot me; I had some difficulty getting home on my own, as there were a lot of sailors in town who kept grabbing at me. When I did eventually arrive home, beyond the fact that Ernie was out looking for me, no one seemed very disturbed that I had come through London on my own, late at night. My aunt's twin daughters, Doris and Annie, acted as waitresses, and my uncle, a quiet and well-spoken man, kept the business side of things.[49] It was marvellous to be able to walk to College – but no situation is perfect. The restaurant was mainly frequented by journalists, and as I had my meals and did my work in the restaurant, it was often a little difficult to concentrate, with the noise of talking and arguing and Ernie's scales and composing going on, quite regardless of any noise going on around him.

One evening I was having some difficulty over my French translation and one of the journalists offered to help me. The next day I was taken to see Miss Braginton by a very irate French mistress. I had to confess to the dubious help I had received and explain about the difficulties I had with my work. She was most kind and understanding and even lent me a handkerchief to wipe my tearful face as I couldn't find mine. I don't suppose I had one. The next day, she informed me that she had arranged for me to do my work in the reading room at the British Museum. I was given a table where the librarian could keep her beady eye on me. When I asked her if I could have a certain book she would get it for me and gave me a pair of white gloves in case I made the pages dirty, and she always inspected my satchel when I went home in case I had filched a book off the shelves when she was not looking. I did a lot of work there and quite enjoyed the atmosphere with the peace and quiet, the rows and rows of books and the men and women reading and writing – many of whom I become quite friendly with.[50]

It was quite exciting going home at the weekend as all the family seemed so pleased to see me. I had to tell them in detail everything I had done during the week, and they told me all their activities, often all talking at the same time. I realised how much I missed them. It seemed as if I was suddenly thrust into an adult world with the journalists in the restaurant, my aunt's family older than myself, the studious men and women in the reading room and the girls in my class at College. I was the youngest in the class and the majority of them seemed so very sophisticated, following the latest fashions, plays and books.

1922 – Examinations

When I was 16 I sat for a Civil Service exam as a junior entrant to one of the Ministries.I found my way to the hall where the exam was to be held, armed with the required pens, nibs and pencils. When I arrived at 8:45 in the morning there seemed to be hundreds of girls pouring out of taxis and motor cars and saying fond farewells to parents. They all seemed to be tall, intelligent-looking and confident, which was more than I was. I grew more and more terrified as the minutes passed.

The doors were opened and we were ushered Into a large room with high ceilings, long windows and couches all round the walls. We were told to hang our hats and coats up in the cloakrooms, which reminded me of school as they had numbers underneath the hooks. I lined up for the lavatory and then trooped back with the others to the waiting room. Soon after nine o'clock the big double doors were opened and the chattering stopped. You could have heard a pin drop. The hall seemed immense, with rows and rows of desks and, hanging from the ceiling in huge letters, was the word "Silence". We were awed and very silent. A young woman stood on either side of the doors and, after asking our name, looked us up on her list and gave us a tab with our name on it which we were instructed to stick on our blouse. There was no sitting next to your best friend. We were taken in tow by another woman who found your desk for you. It also had your name on it. I was very pleased that I had a desk in a row against the wall, which meant that I had a row of girls on one side only. If I could not answer the questions I could at least stare at the wall!

There was a question paper face down on the top of a pad of foolscap. We were told not to turn it over until instructed. I was quite happy to leave mine where it was, until I was told it was English first and we had until 12 o'clock to answer the questions and write an essay. I liked English and soon forgot about the crowds of girls around me, the invigilators walking up and down and the scratching of pens. I scribbled away until we were told we had five minutes to finish. Then we had two hours for lunch and the afternoon session would start at two o'clock. It would be Maths, and I was not so good at Maths.

There was the line of taxis and motor cars and parents waiting to take their chattering daughters to lunch. I stood on the pavement and wondered where to go and felt for the shilling in my pocket. I started to walk down the road when a girl caught up with me, said her name was Helen, she was on her own and could she come with me. I was delighted and we went to a Lyons Corner House which was not far away. Neither of us had much money, so the waitress suggested a pot of tea and a roll with butter and jam. The girl's name was Helen Fountain. She too was a war orphan and the eldest of a large family. Her mother worked all day so couldn't come to London with her. We talked and talked about our families and our ideas, our hopes for the future, and were almost late for the afternoon session. At four o'clock that afternoon it was over. I said goodbye to Helen and she caught her tram and I walked back to Fleet Street. My journalist friends were interested in the exam and I had to tell them all about the papers, particularly the essay titles. They told me which one I should have done and how they would approach it, all different of course, so I kept my ideas to myself.

The term ended and I was invited again to Vaynor Park for my holidays. The family went again to Thaxted where I joined them later. I was at Vaynor Park when a long brown envelope came. I looked at it for some time before opening it. I had never had an official letter addressed to me before. There were a number of sheets of paper with lists of names. I looked for a note from my mother but there was none, so I feared the worst. I had failed and she was cross with me. Two-thirds of the way down the list there was a thick black line so I looked at the names below that with dread in my heart, but Grace Isabelle Lucas was not there so I plucked up courage and started at the top.

Helen Fountain was first on the list and I was pleased I had met her. She was both clever and charming and the two do not often go together. I heard later that she did not accept the position offered to her but went on to university and later became a doctor. I did not envy her but I envied the opportunity. I was eighth on the list and I was overjoyed. The Brigadier and Mrs Corbett-Winder, Millicent and Lettice, John and the staff all came to congratulate me – even the ancient gardener. He took my hand in his gnarled old fist and hoped I would spend it wisely. I think he assumed I had won a lottery – which I suppose I had in a way.

I joined the family in Thaxted as there were still two more weeks of school holidays. They were pleased to see me, full of excited chatter but not unduly impressed with my great achievement. It was apparently only what was expected of me. Bindle put his great paws on my shoulders and pinned me against the wall. This was his usual greeting when I came home from London for weekends. We went out for the whole day and I slept again on the couch with Bindle snoring beside me. Everything was all right again.

There were two letters waiting for me when we got home. One was to tell me when and where I was to go for a medical. The other was a very official-looking form with all the usual things like name and address, age and nationality of my parents, and ancestors back to grandparents, also a list of Ministries. I had to number them in order of preference. Board of Trade, Treasury and such grand places got ticked, and I ignored the Post Office. So what did I get? I got the Post Office. Apparently, that year they were putting the top 20 into the Post Office, as the brightest ones were not ticking it. How right they were, and how much I envied Helen Fountain!

It was then I gave up God and stopped saying my prayers and going to Communion, and started to ask the advice of my big, cheerful, clever father who was buried somewhere in France. I got the answer of course. Every night with my head on a tear-soaked pillow I got the answer "Look after your mother".

The Revd Bayfield Clark came to find out why I was not at Communion so I told him. Everyone told me to work hard and say my prayers, so I did as I

40 *Herne Hill Road c1920.*
   Kemerton Road is the first turning on the left. St Saviour's Church behind

was told and was always let down. I had given up God and was writing poetry instead. I would do as my father wished and look after my mother. My poetry was dreadful and no help at all. A mixture of lost hope, the call of the curlew on a bleak moor and "The Last Post"... so I gave up poetry and went for my medical. Except for being too thin, and of minimum height and weight, I was pronounced fit and went to my first job in the Post Office – and hated it.

Strangely enough, both Dorothy and Gladys followed me to St George's and the Juniors exam for the Civil Service. Dorothy came 40th and was posted to the clerical department of the Central Telegraph Office and Gladys came 35th and went to the Board of Trade. I think the Post Office must have been short of people who could read and write when I went in for that exam. The Civil Service took in such large numbers of bright young girls because they did not employ married women in those days. When you were married you were thrown out with a lump sum charmingly called a "dowry", not redundancy pay. I had £50. I never knew a teacher who was not a Miss, so I suppose the teaching profession was much the same. It was a great scandal to go and live with your boyfriend – so you got married and lost your job.

Over the years I have tried to keep my feet firmly on the ground but my head is often in the clouds.

41 Grace with cat, the only known photo
of her as an adolescent

42 *Grace with her husband Colin*
    at their wedding in 1929

43 *A landscape painting by Grace, undated*

Grace's Life 1920s-2001

Not long after entering work at the Post Office Grace met her future husband, Colin MacFarquhar, at a friend's party. She was still only 16 years old. He was 19 and she thought he was ancient. It would be several years before they married and Grace left the Civil Service with her £50 dowry. She and Colin lived in Eltham Park through the 1930s and it was there that their sons, Gordon and Colin, spent the early years of their childhood.

It was during World War II that Grace returned to the Civil Service, where she served in the Air Ministry and the Ministry of Agriculture. She described the nightmare of working on accounts through the Blitz and walking for miles to get home to her boys, when public transport was severely disrupted. Later, she was moved out of London to continue her duties from a base in the Gloucestershire countryside near to where her sister Dorothy was living.

By some point in the 1940s Grace had moved to Shenfield in Essex, where Gordon and Colin attended Brentwood School and I was born. Gladys had married a farmer and was also settled in Essex, so there were frequent visits between the two families. But not all the siblings lived so near. The two youngest, Fred and Vera, led the most adventurous lives. Fred had migrated to Australia, fought in New Guinea in World War II and later settled in Northern Territory, while Vera travelled the world as a military wife, including periods spent in Egypt, Singapore and Cyprus.

Change came for Grace in 1951, when she moved briefly with the family to Bournemouth and afterwards to the New Forest, where she remained for much of her life. Charlotte, and also Vera and her family, moved to the area some time later. Grace taught for a number of years at a preparatory school outside Lymington. She took a great interest in wildlife and conservation and became president of her village's Women's Institute at Minstead, near Lyndhurst. Throughout her life she retained her enthusiasm for art, was an accomplished amateur watercolour painter and talented dressmaker. Grace was extremely sociable and lively and she made many friends wherever she went.

Her final move was to stay with her son Gordon and family in Herefordshire. She died in July 2001 and is buried in the churchyard at the village of Brampton Bryan.

Elizabeth Sirriyeh (daughter of Grace Lucas)
June 2018

NOTES

Note 1 – *see page 9*

According to the the St Saviour's Parish Magazine (now in London Metro-politan Archives) the World War I memorial in the church listing 99 names was made by James Powell & Sons at the Whitefriars Glassworks, Tudor Street, London EC. The cost was £105. It was officially unveiled by Brigadier General Wray (47th Division, Artillery) in 1920, on the second anniversary of the 11 November Armistice. A Pastoral Scheme was approved in June 1973 rendering St Saviour's redundant and the church was demolished eight years later. The Scheme stated that the contents of the church should be disposed of as the Bishop of Southwark should see fit, but this expressly excluded monuments and memorials. The precise circumstances of the removal of the WWI memorial are not known. Fortunately, the two tablets on each side of a mosaic representation of St George survived and were stored for many years in the basement of the Carnegie Library, until conversion of the library basement into a gym required their removal in 2015 to the Tate Library in Brixton, where they await resto-ration. Sadly, it would seem that the St George centre piece was destroyed, a photograph by M.D. Trace, taken in 1981, being the only known visual record.

Note 2 – *see page 13*

The Lupino theatrical family was extensive, so one cannot say exactly which members of the family Grace might have known. George Hook Lupino (1820-1902) had 16 children, at least 10 of whom became professional entertainers and dancers. One of these was George Lupino (1853-1932), a renowned clown. His sons Barry (1884-1962), Mark (1889-1930) and Stanley (1893-1942) – father of Ida (1918-95) who found fame in Hollywood – all followed the family tradition and became actors and entertainers. At around the time Grace describes father and sons were all living in South London. Stanley, shown in the 1911 Census as a "music hall artiste" aged 17, was living as a boarder at 14 Denmark Road, Camberwell, close to what was to become the Lucas family home at 45 Kemer-ton Road a year or two later. In 1915 Stanley married and moved to Ardbeg Road, Herne Hill. Herne Hill and the surrounding area was popular with music hall performers and residents included, at various times, Dan Leno, Bransby Williams and Marie Loftus.

Note 3 – *see page 15*

Victorian and Edwardian dress included much use of lace, frills, flounces and trimmings, articles that could be detached from a dress or other garment and washed. They then needed to be reshaped with a goffering iron, a cylindrical blade or set of blades that, as with a flat iron, would be heated for this purpose.

Note 4 – *see page 16*

The house that Grace describes was at 45 Kemerton Road. The three-storey terraced house, built c1880, still stands today, at the Herne Hill Road end of the street. Grace dates her earliest memory to 1913 and from what she says the family must have been living at Kemerton Road by that date. At the time of the 1911 Census their home was 38 Havil Street, Camberwell. The family clearly moved around frequently until settling at Kemerton Road. Grace's parents were living in Ealing when they married in 1905; they were living in Iverson Road, Hampstead, when Grace was born the following year; they had moved to Eltham Street, Newington, when Grace's sister Dorothy was born in 1907 and to St George's Road, Camberwell, when her sister Gladys was born in 1909; her brother Fred was born in 1911 at Havil Street. Finally, her sister Vera was born in 1914 at 45 Kemerton Road.

Note 5 – *see page 17*

Grace wrote this memoir some 70 years after the events she describes. Some details are wrong. One can well imagine that Grace's mother would sing popular songs to her children, especially as both her parents had links to music hall artists of the day, but it cannot have been the "Lambeth Walk", which first appeared in 1937 in the musical *Me and My Girl*. The song – and the dance developed for it – was made immensely popular through the entertainer Lupino Lane, who starred in the 1939 film version. He was the first cousin of Stanley Lupino (Note 2 above).

Note 6 – *see page 17*

Grace's mother, Charlotte, was born in Southwark on 27 January 1880, the youngest of seven children. Her parents were Thomas Finch and Elizabeth Finch (née Boyd). Charlotte's father, a dustman, died when she was only nine months old (not before she was born, as Grace goes on to say). The 1881 Census shows Elizabeth widowed, aged 37, and living with her four younger children, including Charlotte, in Zoar Street, Southwark and working as an artificial-flower maker. In the days before pensions and social security working class women who were widowed had no option but to find work, while at the same time somehow caring for their children. It made sense to remarry in these circumstances, which Elizabeth did in 1888. It is interesting to note that when Elizabeth was first married she could only leave her "mark" on the marriage register. Her husband was likewise illiterate. But when she marries again she is able to sign her name, though her husband is not. Charlotte's early life must have been an unending struggle to make ends meet. It is no surprise that Charlotte was implacably opposed to Grace's later ambition to go to art school. An education that would provide a reliable job and decent wage was all that mattered.

Note 7 – *see page 17*

Grace's grandmother (Fred Lucas's mother) was not French and she was not called Isabelle. In an age when, for most people, family history was handed down orally, with few if any documents to look to, it is easy to see how family myths can arise. Such stories may well have some grain of truth in them, though in this case it has not been possible to locate any French element on the Lucas side of the family. Grace's grandmother was in fact born Caroline Quarrington (there are various spellings) in 1854 in Aston Clinton, Buckinghamshire. Both Caroline's parents came from that county. Fred Lucas's sister was called Isabel, the spelling in the official registration of her birth, though "Isabelle" is used on the registration of her marriage in 1902 and she signed with that spelling. There is more about Fred Lucas in the Introduction.

Note 8 – *see page 18*

Grace's maternal grandmother died in December 1896. Grace's mother, Charlotte, would have been 16, not 13. It also seems more likely that Charlotte had already left school by the time she was 16 and was having to earn a living. The 1901 Census shows Charlotte employed as an ironer in a laundry.

Note 9 – *see page 19*

The Belle of New York was a musical comedy with libretto by Charles McLellan (writing under the name "Hugh Morton") and Gustave Kerker. It was first staged, to limited acclaim, in New York in 1897. It transferred the next year to London, where it became huge hit and ran for more than a year. It also enjoyed great success in other European capitals, was revived many times in the West End and saw numerous amateur productions.

Note 10 – *see page 19*

Fred Karno, born Frederick John Westcott (1866-1941), was a stage acrobat who went on to become a highly successful music hall impresario. He is remembered particularly for spotting the talents of Charlie Chaplin and Stan Laurel. They toured with the Karno troupe in America and, as music hall began to fade, stayed to make their fortune in films. In his heyday Karno staged many shows running at the same time in London and elsewhere and, requiring a base for storing stage sets and props and for rehearsing the shows, he converted houses in Southwell Road, Camberwell, for the purpose. The curious four-storey "Fun Factory" at No. 38 survives to this day (now Clockwork Studios), a short distance from the Lucas family home in Kemerton Road. Karno himself lived very close to his Fun Factory at 28 Vaughan Road. The mayhem and slapstick of Karno's shows became a byword for chaotic merriment. Amidst the miseries of the trenches soldiers would sing, to the tune of the hymn "The Church's One Foundation":

We are Fred Karno's army, we are the ragtime infantry.
We cannot fight, we cannot shoot, what bleeding use are we?
And when we get to Berlin we'll hear the Kaiser say,
Hoch, hoch! Mein Gott, what a bloody rotten lot, are the ragtime infantry.

Note 11 – *see page 19*

Lottie Collins (1865-1910) was a music hall singer and dancer. She was the first performer in Britain of the American song "Ta-ra-ra Boom-de-ay". Her performance was considered by some as risqué but it secured her fame. The song survives to this day, especially in parodic versions by schoolchildren.

Note 12 – *see page 20*

The term "bassinet" is used today, especially in the US and Australia, to describe a lightweight cradle for a baby. In the period Grace describes "bassinette" or "bassinette perambulator" was widely used for what today would be called a pram.

Note 13 – *see page 20*

Grace was not alone in thinking that one of the best-known propaganda posters of all time – Lord Kitchener with pointed finger and the words "Your Country Needs You!" – was everywhere to be seen as the country mobilised for war. The popular belief is that it played a key role in helping Kitchener, Secretary of State for War, raise the huge volunteer army, known as "Kitchener's Army" or the "New Army", that was needed as soon as war was declared on 4 August

1914. The famous image did appear on the cover of the magazine *London Opinion* in September 1914, but it was not used in official posters and there is no evidence that it enjoyed extensive circulation. There was a widely used official poster at the start of the war featuring Kitchener, but it had no pointing finger, piercing eyes or strong message. Instead it contained the less than inspiring: "Lord Kitchener says: Men, materials and money are the immediate necessities. Does the call of duty find no response in you until reinforced – let us rather say superseded – by the call of compulsion? Enlist Today". In contrast, Alfred Leete, the graphic artist who designed the "Your Country Needs You" image, understood how to create a picture with concise wording of compelling power, one that has been often imitated.

Note 14 – *see page 23*

The BL (breech loading) 9.2-inch howitzer was a heavy siege howitzer, first tested at Rhayader in Wales in July 1914, brought into service in France three months later and nicknamed "Mother". It was considered to be a huge improvement on existing siege artillery. The example in the Imperial War Museum is, apart from the carriage, the first model built and initially the only one in use. Further production guns became available in 1915. By the end of the war about 450 of these howitzers had been brought into service. The total weight of the gun was 41 tons. This assisted its stability and accuracy in firing, but moving and re-assembly was laborious. It could be pulled in a train of three carriages by a team of 12 heavy horses or by a motorised tractor. One of the most striking war memorials to be seen in London is the Grade I-listed Royal Artillery Memorial at Hyde Park Corner (see Illustration 3). The sculptural work by Charles Jagger includes a 9.2 inch howitzer carved from Portland stone, larger than life size and modelled on the example in the Imperial War Museum.

Note 15 – *see page 23*

The house at 45 Kemerton Road did not have a garden that backed onto Ruskin Park, but Ruskin Park would have been visible from the top of the house. And Grace may have known children in houses at the far end of Kemerton Road/ Finsen Road or in Herne Hill Road. These houses did have gardens backing onto the park.

Note 16 – *see page 24*

Grace is correct in remembering Will Scenling, though he was 18 when he died of wounds in France, 10 days after the end of the war. The Scenling family lived at 12 Herne Hill Road, close to the Lucas home. Will was the oldest of four children. His name is commemorated on the St Saviour's memorial. It has not been possible to trace Jack Crawford.

Note 17 – *see page 24*

On Christmas Eve 1914 a German seaplane dropped a bomb on Dover. It was the very first time that a bomb fell from the air over England. Zeppelin raids began a month later over East Anglia. In May 1915 they reached London. The country was entirely unprepared in terms of warnings or precautions, though over time this improved. In an age before radar, warnings were dependent on visual observation of aircraft as they crossed the coast and moved inland. To accurately plot the course of Zeppelins when they were flying as high as two miles, often in darkness and with cloud cover, was exceptionally difficult. Observations were telephoned in to London and analysed. The priority was to give reliable information to aircrews, which from 1916 onwards were sent up to engage the enemy. For the civilian population warnings were disseminated by telephone messages to police stations around the capital. To spread the word, police officers – and, as Grace describes, civilian volunteers – would then patrol the streets on foot, bicycle or car, using whistles, rattles or sometimes bugles, to attract attention and armed with placards proclaiming "Take Cover" and, when the danger was thought to have passed, "All Clear". In terms of morale it was important that Londoners felt something was being done to protect them; in practice it was of limited value. There were no purpose-built air raid shelters, only cellars, railway arches and large buildings, none of which were very safe. Underground stations were widely used, and probably the safest. The limitations of visual observation worked both ways. Zeppelins often had no accurate idea where they were and bombs could be dropped quite randomly, as seen in this parody from 1916 of the moralising verse "How doth the busy little bee …":

How doth the busy Zeppelin
Improve each foggy night?
It drops a bomb on Camberwell
And hits the Isle of Wight.

Note 18 – *see page 24*

Defence against air raids was virtually non-existent at the start of the war. There were no purpose-built anti-aircraft guns. Artillery weapons were simply upended and pointed at the sky. Generally, the Zeppelins were at a height beyond the range of these guns. No Zeppelins were brought down in

1915, whether by anti-aircraft fire or aeroplanes. In that year there were just 12 fixed position anti-aircraft batteries in the built-up area of London. In the course of 1916 this increased five-fold and by 1917 the number of men engaged in air defence at home had grown to about 17,000. There was growing success, through improvements in training and technology and increase in resources, in the shooting down of enemy airships and aeroplanes, which led to the cessation of Zeppelin raids after October 1917 and of attacks by Gotha and Giant bombers after May 1918. Grace's recollection of a gun emplacement in Ruskin Park is corroborated in the recollection of another local resident, Bert Goodes. It is also the case that there was a battery of 12 anti-aircraft guns on ground next to James Allen's Girls School. They were still there, covered up and guarded by an officer and five soldiers – apparently with nothing else to do – in July 1920. Since Grace attended the school after the war she must have been aware of them. In *The Defence of London 1915-18* by A. Rawlinson (1923), an authoritative account of London's air defence, the map at p.162 shows an anti-aircraft emplacement at Dulwich, but none in Ruskin Park, though it does show a searchlight in what could be the park.

Note 19 – *see page 24*

Grace's recollection of a Zeppelin in flames and visible from the house in Kemerton Road must be treated with scepticism. Some Zeppelins were brought down, but there is no record of one coming down over South-east London. The downing of enemy aircraft had huge propaganda value; it is therefore very unlikely that such an event would go unrecorded. Probably the most widely reported – and observed by vast numbers of Londoners at the time – was the fate of Zeppelin SL11 in September 1916, shot down by 2nd Lieutenant William Leefe Robinson over North London and crashing in flames, with no survivors, at Cuffley in Hertfordshire. Robinson became a national hero overnight and just two days later – a record – was awarded the Victoria Cross by King George V.

Note 20 – *see page 26*

Home & Colonial Stores were one of the largest food retailers in Britain in the first half of the last century. The company grew from one store in Edgware in 1883 to 500 two decades later and more than 3,000 in the 1930s. The brand name disappeared in 1961. The Home & Colonial closest to the Lucas family home would have been at 220 Coldharbour Lane (Illustration 22). There was another store opposite Herne Hill station at 218 Railton Road, next to The Commercial pub.

Note 21 – *see page 26*

Grace's recollection here confuses what she came to know subsequently and what she became aware of during the war. She is right about the long lists of casualties. It would have been difficult to suppress this information. However, it was never presented with any reference to the physical suffering endured at the Front, but in the positive glow of heroic sacrifice and patriotic duty. Newspapers did not report, in any truthful sense, on conditions in the trenches. Indeed they were prevented from doing so. Within days of the outbreak of war DORA (the Defence of the Realm Act) laid down in law that "No person shall by word of mouth or in writing spread reports likely to cause disaffection or alarm among any of His Majesty's forces or among the civilian population". The news that was published was often highly misleading, particularly through the omission of bad news. For example, reading reports in the days following 1 July 1916 – the opening of the Somme offensive and the most catastrophic single day in British military history, with more than 60,000 British soldiers killed and wounded – one would think that the failed advance had been a solid success. It was in these early days of the Somme offensive that Grace's father died. News of the true conditions at the front did leak out, rarely from the letters that were written home, which were subject to censorship, but from men returning wounded or on leave. There was, however, no press willing or able to bring such individual stories together and present the reality to a wide audience. That was precisely what the government wanted. As Prime Minister Lloyd George famously admitted in 1917 to C.P. Scott, editor of the Manchester Guardian, "If people really knew [the truth], the war would be stopped tomorrow. But of course they don't know, and can't know."

Note 22 – *see page 27*

Mrs Longman's confectionary shop was at 42 Kemerton Road, just three doors down from the Lucas home. The numbering in Kemerton Road was, and is, continuous.

Note 23 – *see page 29*

Grace is correct in remembering a family called Bruggemeyer. They lived at 3 Kemerton Road, opposite the Lucas house. The 1911 Census shows William and Florence Bruggemeyer, aged 50 and 43. William (1860-1927) was an overseer in the General Post Office. They had four daughters and a son living with them, aged between 21 and 10. Their eldest daughter, Ellen, was a schoolteacher employed by the London County Council. Her sister Annie was a year younger. Both parents and all the children were born in London. William Bruggemeyer's parents were Dutch-born. It has not been possible to find evidence of any connection to Germany, as Grace remembers. The Bruggemeyer son, William Charles (born 1899), served in the army and was gassed in the eyes and hospitalised in September 1918. In later life he became an osteopath and had his practice for many years at 99 Herne Hill. It is still an osteopath's surgery today.

Note 24 – *see page 31*

The walk to Camberwell Green would have taken the family along Coldharbour Lane. Illustration 24 shows what they could have seen. The build-ings are still there today, though the shop fronts have changed.

Note 25 – *see page 32*

There was no school directly on Coldharbour Lane. The London County Council school at Crawford Street, Camberwell, just off Coldharbour Lane, would seem the most likely destination for Grace. In comparison to the small Church school next to St Saviour's, which was literally round the corner, the walk to Crawford Street would have seemed a great deal longer.

Note 26 – *see page 34*

John Bayfield Clark was the Vicar of St Saviour's. Born in 1855, he would have been aged about 62 at the time Grace describes. He was educated at Marlborough College and Cambridge and became the Vicar of St Saviour's in 1891, remaining there for 37 years until his retirement. The 1911 Census shows him as unmarried but living with his sister Margaret, a widow with no children, and three domestic servants. Grace was clearly right in her memory of some-thing rather grand in the Vicar's lifestyle, for the vicarage contained 11 rooms. But the Vicar as husband of the Bishop of London's daughter derives from her own imagination or, equally probably, a story that children in the area devised to fit the "stately and severe" lady at the vicarage. It is also possible that Grace is remembering the lady who became Mrs Bayfield Clark, but only in 1920. The Vicar married Mary Corysande Streatfeild at St George's Hanover Square. She was not the Bishop of London's daughter. An insight into how times have changed in the Church of England can be found in the fact that in 1911, while the unmarried Reverend Bayfield Clark lived comfortably on Herne Hill Road, the Bishop of London, Arthur Winnington-Ingram, likewise unmarried, enjoyed an official residence at 32 St James's Square, Westminster. It comprised 28 rooms, which the Bishop shared with his chaplain, his private secretary and no fewer than 10 servants. Winnington-Ingram is best remembered today for his zealous advocacy of the war- a position, it should be said, he shared with almost every other member of the British establishment. In 1915, when preaching at Westminster Abbey, his sermon included the exhortation that all "who love freedom and honour are banded in a great crusade – we cannot deny it – to kill Germans; to kill them, not for the sake of killing, but to save the world; to kill the good as well as the bad, to kill the young as well as the old... and to kill them lest the civilisation of the world itself be killed... As I have said a thousand times, I look upon it as a war for purity, I look upon everyone who dies in it as a martyr".

Note 27 – *see page 36*

There is no record of a bomb falling on Ruskin Park during the First World War, though there are cases of German aircraft aiming bombs at anti-aircraft stations. It seems there was an anti-aircraft station in the park and at North Dulwich (see Note 17). Instances of bombs landing on Camberwell, Brixton, Peckham and Dulwich are documented. A report issued by the London Fire Brigade in 1919 refers to Herne Hill being bombed on one occasion but, assuming that is right, the precise location or locations seem not to have been recorded.

Note 28 – *see page 42*

Andrew Carnegie (1835-1919) was the Scottish-born industrialist who in his later years ensured that his huge fortune, many billions in today's terms, was given away in the advancement of social and educational projects, not least the building of public libraries in many parts of the English-speaking world, open to all and free of charge. The Carnegie Library in Herne Hill, a fine Grade II-listed building that still stands today, was opened in 1906, the year Grace was born. At that time, and until after the First World War, the land at the top of Herne Hill Road was not built up as it is today. Similarly, Red Post Hill, a lane leading from the top of Denmark Hill/Herne Hill down to Dulwich was still rural in appearance. The Sunray Estate on either side of Red Post Hill only appeared in 1920/21. Grace is technically incorrect in saying that the library was at the top of Red Post Hill – it was towards the top of Herne Hill Road, but the essence of her recollection is correct.

Note 29 – *see page 43*

The St Saviour's Parish Magazine states that Confirmation on 28 April 1918 was conducted by the Rt Revd W.W. Hough Bishop of Woolwich, not the Bishop of London. So too the following year. See also Note 26.

Note 30 – *see page 44*

See also Notes 18 and 19. The final Zeppelin raid on London occurred on 19/20 October 1917. In that raid six of the 13 airships that set out were lost. In January 1918 a disastrous fire at the Naval Airship Division's base near Bremen destroyed five more, plus several of the massive hangars that housed them. These setbacks brought Zeppelin raids over London to an end. Bombing from aeroplanes, a far more effective means of delivering death and destruction, had begun in June 1917; these continued and posed a greater potential danger to London's population. As the tide of the war turned, the raids declined, the last on London occurring on 19 May 1918. However, it is the Zeppelin, both at the time and in the years since, that has exercised the more powerful influence on the popular imagination. It clearly did so in Grace's case, as one sees in her earlier vivid recollection of witnessing a Zeppelin in flames.

Note 31 – *see page 44*

It is not surprising that Grace remembers the sight of casualties. Her home was close to King's College Hospital. The hospital had moved out from Central London to its new home on Denmark Hill in 1913. To treat and care for the huge number of casualties brought back from the Front, hospitals all over London were turned over, wholly or in part, to military use. King's became the 4th London General Hospital, accommodating some 300 officers and 1,600 other ranks. Temporary buildings were also erected in Ruskin Park to house convalescent patients. Just up the road from King's the large house on Denmark Hill, once the home of Sir Henry Bessemer, was given over by its owner Sir William Vestey to the War Office for hospital use. And in Camberwell, at Myatt's Fields, St Gabriel's College and the London Board school next to it became the 1st London General Hospital; it was here that Vera Brittain served as a nurse, experiences recorded in *Testament of Youth*, which included feeling the vibrations of the massive artillery bombardment that preceded the Somme offensive in July 1916.

Note 32 – *see page 46*

Grace may be confusing the chronology here, in that by this time she herself had left the small church school at St Saviour's and had moved on to a senior school, probably the LCC school at Crawford Road, Camberwell. Or she could be remembering what other children, including her sister Gladys, told her about what was going on in the playground.

Note 33 – *see page 46*

See Note 23. The only resident with German nationality that it has been possible to trace in Kemerton Road is Henri Klasmeier, a tailor. The 1911 Census shows him at No.15 with his English-born wife and two young children, both born in Herne Hill. As a German national Mr Klasmeier would have been interned. It is interesting to note that the St Saviour's Parish Magazine for August 1917 not only records a medal "for industry, attendance and conduct" for Grace's sister Gladys in Class IV at St Saviour's School but also one for Florrie Klasmeier in Class II. She was the elder of the Klasmeiers' two children, baptised at St Saviour's in 1904 (where her father is named as Heinrich, not Henri, Klasmeier). Mrs Klasmeier and her two children can be traced in London after the war but the fate of Mr Klasmeier is not known. There were many German immigrants working in London before World War I, typically as tailors, hairdressers, bakers and waiters – in the Herne Hill area, far more than any other foreign nationals.

Note 34 – *see page 46*

It seems probable that this was Dr George Cooper MB ChB, who lived at 168 Coldharbour Lane, at the junction with Luxor Street, a few minutes' walk from Kemerton Road. There is no other Dr Cooper in the 1919 Post Office Directory from the Herne Hill/Camberwell/Brixton area.

Note 35 – *see page 47*

Bay rum is an oil distilled from the leaves of the bay tree. Mixed with other ingredients it became a staple hair tonic from the mid-19th century, largely through the work of the Danish chemist and businessman A.H. Riise, working from St Thomas, then a Danish colony in the West Indies. It is still marketed today. Cantharides derives from an irritating substance, cantharidin, secreted by blister beetles, so called because contact causes blistering of the human skin. It was widely thought that this reaction could stimulate hair growth, a theory that finds no support today. The ingestion of cantharides, once reputed as an aphrodisiac (popularly known as "Spanish fly") is also now discouraged, not least because the toxicity can prove fatal in excessive doses. Preparations of bay rum said to also contain cantharides were certainly available in 1918, though whether they actually did so is questionable.

Note 36 – *see page 48*

Grace describes two card games popular with children. "Beat Your Neighbour out of Doors" is also known as "Beggar My Neighbour", the aim of which is to win all the cards in the pack. "Old Maid" is played with a pack from which one Queen has been removed and the aim is not to be left as the player with an unpaired Queen in your hand: Gladys's fate.

Note 37 – *see page 48*

"The Farmer Wants a Wife" is a traditional nursery rhyme, used by children for a playground game. It progresses from the "the farmer wants a wife to "the wife wants a child", "the child wants a nurse", "the nurse wants a dog", "we all pat the dog" etc. The children sing the rhyme as they hold hands and dance around one child, the farmer. Others in the ring break off one by one and join the farmer in the centre of the ring as wife, child, nurse, dog etc.

Note 38 – *see page 48*

Cinderella was the pantomime at the Theatre Royal Drury Lane that opened in 1919, not 1918 (although it was the 1918 pantomime at the Lyceum). Grace's earlier reference to getting free tickets for many years at Drury Lane would suggest her recollection is of the 1919 *Cinderella* production. It starred the Edwardian beauty Florence Smithson, the "Welsh Nightingale" (Illustration 32), as Cinderella and Stanley Lupino as Buttons.

Note 39 – *see page 49*

It is not known how Grace's father was known to Captain – as Grace describes him – Corbett-Winder. William Corbett-Winder in fact held the rank of Major at this time. He was born in 1875 and served in the Army before the war. In 1902 he is listed as a Captain in the 4th Battalion of the South Wales Borderers, transferring in 1908 to the 7th (Montgomery and Merionethshire) Battalion, Royal Welsh Fusiliers. This battalion went out to Egypt in 1915 and took part, at very heavy cost, in the Gallipoli landings, but was not sent to France. William Corbett-Winder married Margery Bardwell at St Saviour's Church, Knightsbridge, in 1906 and inherited the Vaynor Park estate upon the death of his father the following year.

Note 40 – *see page 49*

The Corbett-Winders were, and remain today, a family established over many generations at Vaynor Park in Montgomeryshire (since 1974 a county subsumed within Powys). Vaynor Park, the house, is a Grade II*-listed building, and described as "a major country house of exceptional quality, as a substantial early C17 brick house (one of a very small number in the county) which was the subject of a major mid C19 re-modelling itself of considerable historical interest for its Renaissance Revival detail. The quality of the interiors is also exceptional." The garden and landscape setting are also very fine.

Note 41 – *see page 50*
The two Corbett-Winder daughters were called Violet Millicent (though she was known by her second name) and Venice. Millicent was about the same age as Grace and Venice some two years younger. Grace, incorrectly, refers to her as "Lettice". The youngest child was John Lyon Corbett-Winder, born 1911, the same age as Grace's brother Freddie. Grace calls John Lyon "John", but he was always known by his second name "Lyon".

Note 42 – *see page 51*
The person Grace remembers as the "Brigadier" cannot have been the father of her host, William Corbett-Winder. His father had died in 1907. He did have a brother, also in the army, Captain Frederick Feilden Corbett-Winder, and this is perhaps the gentleman Grace recalls. It is also possible that it was Captain Frederick Corbett-Winder who made contact with Grace and travelled with her from London and that the "Brigadier" was Major William Corbett-Winder, father of the three children Grace remembers.

Note 43 – *see page 51*
There is – and was – no pub called the Green Dragon in Berriew. Montgomery, a few miles away, has the historic Dragon Hotel. This could account for Grace's confusion of the name.

Note 44 – *see page 51*
Violet Ida Eveline Herbert, Countess of Powis and 16th Baroness Darcy de Knayth (a title she held in her own right) was married to the 5th Earl of Powis. Their home was at the medieval Powis Castle, near Welshpool and some five miles from Vaynor Park. Lady Powis (1865-1929) is remembered for her trans-formation of the gardens at Powis Castle, today amongst the finest in Wales. She lost her eldest son Percy Robert Herbert, Viscount Clive in 1916. He died in hospital in London, 18 days after being wounded at the Battle of the Somme. Grace's father had died of wounds in the same battle two months earlier. Powis

Castle passed to the National Trust after the death of the 5th Earl in 1952.

Note 45 – *see page 52*

Illustration 38 shows Fred Lucas's six medals. They comprise (from left to right): 1. Military Medal, gazetted in the London Gazette on 16 February 1917. There was no central register for MM awards and neither the war diary of Fred's unit nor his own personal war service record have survived; so it is not possible to say with certainty why the medal was awarded, though Fred's family believes it may be linked to Fred's engineering skills in improving the performance of armaments. The reverse has the words "For Bravery in the Field". 2. Queen's South Africa Medal with three battle clasps, Transvaal – Cape Colony – Orange Free State. 3. Kings South Africa Medal with date clasps, South Africa 1901 and South Africa 1902. 4. 1914-15 Star Medal, awarded to officers and men of British and Imperial forces who served against the Central European Powers in any theatre of the war between 5 August 1914 and 31 December 1915, thus in all cases before conscription was introduced. 5. The British War Medal. The reverse, shows Saint George naked on horseback and armed with a short sword. The horse tramples on the Prussian eagle shield and the emblems of death, a skull and cross-bones. 6. The Victory Medal. The reverse has the words "The Great War for Civilisation 1914–1919".

Note 46 – *see page 52*

The imposing Garrison Church of St George was designed by Thomas Henry Wyatt and built in 1862-63 as the church for the Royal Artillery, whose barracks were at the opposite end of the regiment's extensive parade ground. Sadly, the church was largely destroyed by bombs in 1944, though some of the walls and decorative elements of the chancel survived and have been restored in recent times and are now protected beneath a new roof. Army re-organisation has meant the Royal Artillery are, after 300 years, no longer housed at Woolwich. Other regiments, following the sell-off of the St John's Wood and Chelsea bar-racks for luxury housing, have been using the historic Woolwich barracks, but the Ministry of Defence have announced that they will be disposed of in 2028.

Note 47 – *see page 54*

St George's College was a college that offered courses to both men and women – but in separate premises – across a broad area; in particular, prepara-tion for the Civil Service examinations. Its founder was William Braginton (1844-1922), not the Master of King's College London as Grace thought, but the Dean of the Civil Service Department of King's. He also started the evening classes that developed into a successful full-time school, becoming known as the Strand School and housed in the basement of King's. He was its headmaster until 1913, when the school moved to Elm Park, Tulse Hill, a popular grammar school until its closure in 1979. William Braginton was not the brother – as Grace thought – but the father of Sophia Braginton (1868-1938), the eldest of eight daughters. She was one of the first women to study at Cambridge and became a lecturer in the Civil Service Department at King's College. It took the University of Cambridge until 1948 to grant full degrees for women students – up to then they could only receive a form of certificate. This did not prevent Miss Braginton from using the title MA in the regular press advertisements for St George's College, of which she became the principal after her father's death. Red Lion Square was very badly damaged by bombs in 1941. St George's College disappeared in the rebuilding after the war.

Note 48 – *see page 54*

See Note 7 with regard to Grace's "French" grandmother.

Note 49 – *see page 55*

Grace is right about the names of her five cousins, but the 1911 Census shows Ernest as aged four, and therefore about her own age and not older; the two youngest, Doris and Annie, were not twins but two and a half years apart. Her uncle, Frank Hopwood Middleton, is shown as a refreshment caterer. The family at this date were living at Westcliff-on-Sea, Essex.

Note 50 – *see page 55*

From the description Grace gives of the library and given the Bragintons' close connection with King's College, it seems more likely that Grace used King's or another university library rather than the British Museum Reading Room for study.

Acknowledgements

As described in the Introduction, *Grace's Story* came into being through our Lottery-Funded project "Remembering Herne Hill 1914-18". Staff Serjeant Frederick Lucas, the father of the author of this memoir, was just one of hundreds of casualties who lived in Herne Hill or had strong Herne Hill connections.

There is no civic memorial in Herne Hill to commemorate all those killed in the First World War, and at the time of writing the final figure is still not known. To find out about the men whose lives and deaths we have investigated and recorded, visit the Herne Hill Society's First World War website **memorial.hernehillsociety.org.uk**

The project continues. At time of writing we are investigating the stories of other residents who lived through the war, including many of German origin.

We should like to take this opportunity to thank all the volunteers – both school students and adults – who helped to compile the website or helped in other ways. John Conway, our website designer, and Dan Townsend, Head of History at our project partners the Charter School North Dulwich, deserve special mention. We have received encouragement and practical assistance from Karen Brookfield, Victoria Moralo and Anne Young at the Heritage Lottery Fund; Helen Hayes MP; Jon Newman, Len Reilly and Susan Shanks at Lambeth Archives, Calista Lucy at Dulwich College Archives, Elen Curran at James Allen's Girls' School and Nicola Waddington at Alleyn's School Archives; Professor Michael Roper, Professor Jerry White and Dan Hill; Tom Harper at the British Library; David Statham and Kevin Chik of Southeastern Railway; William Corbett-Winder and Rosemary Gosling; John Brunton; and the Committees of both the Herne Hill Society and the Herne Hill Forum. Particular thanks go to Sophia Marsh for her time and skill in designing and laying out this book.

Above all we are indebted to Fred Lucas's grand-daughters, Elizabeth Sirriyeh in England and Frankie Maclean in Australia, who enabled us to discover Grace's memoir and without whose generosity and assistance this publication would not have been possible.